Committee for a Strategic Transportation Research Study: Highway Safety

SPECIAL REPORT 229

Safety Research for a Changing Highway Environment

Strategic Transportation Research Study: Highway Safety

TRANSPORTATION RESEARCH BOARD
National Research Council
Washington, D.C. 1990

Transportation Research Board Special Report 229

Subscriber Category
IVB   safety and human performance

Mode
1   highway transportation

Subject areas
11   administration
12   planning
51   transportation safety
52   human factors

Transportation Research Board publications are available by ordering directly from TRB. They may also be obtained on a regular basis through organizational or individual affiliation with TRB; affiliates or library subscribers are eligible for substantial discounts. For further information, write to the Transportation Research Board, National Research Council, 2101 Constitution Avenue, N.W., Washington, D.C. 20418.

Printed in the United States of America

NOTICE: The project that is the subject of this report was approved by the Governing Board of the National Research Council, whose members are drawn from the councils of the National Academy of Sciences, the National Academy of Engineering, and the Institute of Medicine. The members of the committee responsible for the report were chosen for their special competencies and with regard for appropriate balance.

This report has been reviewed by a group other than the authors according to the procedures approved by a Report Review Committee consisting of the members of the National Academy of Sciences, the National Academy of Engineering, and the Institute of Medicine.

This report was sponsored by the Federal Highway Administration and the National Highway Traffic Safety Administration of the U.S. Department of Transportation.

Library of Congress Cataloging-in-Publication Data

Safety research for a changing highway environment: strategic transportation research study: highway safety.
   p. cm.—(Special report ; 229) ISBN 0-309-05056-1
   1. Transportation, Automotive—Safety measures—Research—United States.
   2. Traffic safety—Research—United States. I. National Research Council (U.S.). Transportation Research Board. II. Series: Special report (National Research Council (U.S.). Transportation Research Board); 229.
HE5614.2.S24   1990
363.12′5′0973—dc20   ISSN 0360-859X   90-19676
                                                                        CIP

Cover design: Karen White

Cover photographs:

top left, Dan A. Rosen, TRB; *top right,* Herbert A. Pennock, TRB; *bottom,* Sergio Rodriguez, Davie, Florida.

Preface

In the next 10 to 15 years, many new safety features, such as airbags and antilock brakes, will become standard equipment on passenger vehicles, further improving the safety of motor vehicle travel. These new safety features are the product of years of research and development, and, in the case of airbags, of lengthy regulatory controversy over their implementation. The process of introducing new safety improvements thus requires a long lead time before the full benefits of the improvements in saving lives and reducing injuries are realized.

Is the groundwork being laid for developing a new generation of safety improvements to address tomorrow's safety problems? Over the next several decades, the safety of motor vehicle travel is likely to be affected adversely by a growing population of older drivers and pedestrians, an increasing mix of large trucks and small passenger vehicles, and an aging highway infrastructure. Fortunately, although there is no single countermeasure to eliminate highway injuries, continuing improvements are possible. The vehicle can be designed to protect occupants better in a crash; more can be done to pinpoint, and then relieve, the instances in which the driver makes an error; and the highway itself can be designed to be less hazardous.

The purpose of this study is to examine how well the highway safety research community is prepared to address these emerging safety problems and to capitalize on opportunities for their solution. To carry out this task, the Transportation Research Board (TRB) formed a committee of 15 specialists in highway safety and research management under the leadership of Ray Chamberlain, Executive Director of the Colorado Department of Highways. The committee included experts on human factors and driver behavior, driver licensing and enforcement, highway design, safety program administration, vehicle design and engineering, public health and emergency medicine, countermeasure evaluation, and economics. The members represent a wide range of organizations involved in conducting or using highway safety research, including state highway and transportation departments, state departments of motor vehicles, universities and consultants, the insurance industry, automobile manufacturers and suppliers, and highway user groups. The results of the committee's year-long deliberations are summarized in a package of recommendations for improving the scope, funding, and management of future highway safety research activities.

Nancy Humphrey managed the study and, with Stephen Godwin and Thomas Menzies, drafted the final report under the guidance of the committee and the overall supervision of Robert E. Skinner, Jr., Director for Special Projects. Richard Pain provided significant assistance in reviewing drafts of the manuscript. The Director and staff of the Office of Driver and Pedestrian Research at the National Highway Traffic Safety Administration made significant contributions to the historical overview of driver-related research programs. Members of TRB's technical committees in the highway safety area also offered many valuable suggestions for promising research topics. Special appreciation is expressed to Marguerite Schneider and Frances Holland for assistance in typing drafts of the manuscript.

Contents

Executive Summary

M otor vehicle crashes are a leading cause of death and injury in the United States. The annual drain on society's resources is enormous—$70 billion (in 1986 dollars) in lost productivity, medical costs, and property damage. These monetary losses are comparable with those from cancer and heart disease. In the recently released National Transportation Policy, the U.S. Secretary of Transportation stated his commitment to reducing the costly toll from death and injury on the nation's highways and targeted safety as a top departmental priority.

Achieving a reduction in deaths and injuries from traffic crashes will be difficult. Continued growth in motor vehicle travel and expected changes in the travel environment—more older drivers and pedestrians, more large-truck travel, greater disparity in vehicle size and weight, and a more congested and aging highway infrastructure—are likely to raise the number of deaths and injuries on the highways in the coming decades. New technologies with the potential to provide drivers with additional information and automate certain driving functions are being developed as part of the work on intelligent vehicle-highway systems (IVHS); however, the effect of these technologies on safety is not known. Research provides the means to develop measures to counter emerging safety problems and evaluate opportunities for safety gains.

The Federal Highway Administration (FHWA) and the National Highway Traffic Safety Administration (NHTSA) jointly funded a Strategic Transportation Research Study for Highway Safety to assess the adequacy of current research programs to take the lead in improving the nation's safety record. A special committee of the Transportation Research Board, which carried out the study, reviewed the scope, direction, and funding of highway safety research programs and gave special attention to ways that the process of conducting research could be improved to encourage innovation and quality of scholarship.

Research has played a vital role in developing and evaluating the key safety improvements of the last several decades, yet the research effort has

1

declined during the 1980s. Cutbacks in federal funding have reduced support for research at NHTSA and FHWA, the primary federal sponsors of highway safety research. Funding for state-sponsored research is spread thin. A more troubling factor has been reduced support for training new researchers, leaving too few qualified scientists to conduct needed long-term research. Moreover, the scarce funds that are available are not allocated effectively; they are constrained by program and project goals that are often narrowly defined and contracting methods that limit researchers' scope of inquiry.

The upcoming congressional reauthorization of the safety research budgets for NHTSA and FHWA in the Highway Safety Act and the National Traffic and Motor Vehicle Safety Act provides an opportunity to reverse these trends. Specifically, the committee recommends:

- The rebuilding and sustaining of programs of long-term research in the mission agencies;
- Additional annual federal funding of $30 million to $40 million (in 1990 dollars), growing annually at 5 to 7 percent in real terms over the next 5 to 10 years, to support long-term research programs and build the necessary research infrastructure (this recommended funding level would be higher but for the lack of available qualified scientists to conduct the research);
- Use of the recommended additional resources to support a program that emphasizes peer-reviewed, investigator-initiated research; multiyear funding of research programs; more flexible funding arrangements; and education and training of new researchers;
- Enhanced funding of biomechanics research by the U.S. Department of Transportation (DOT), concentrated in no more than two university centers because of the high capital investment costs, to provide the knowledge base for further advances in injury reduction;
- Support for three to five university centers specializing in human factors and other highway safety research disciplines to advance the knowledge of effective crash avoidance strategies; and
- A new cooperative program for state-sponsored highway safety research to stimulate more joint state research on driver- and vehicle-related issues.

ROLE OF RESEARCH IN HIGHWAY SAFETY

Motor vehicle crashes claim about 45,000 lives, including a disproportionate share of young lives, and cause nearly 4 million injuries each year. These crashes are the leading cause of injury and the sixth leading cause of death in the United States. The annual burden to society of the lost productivity of crash victims, the medical costs of injured survivors, and the property damage to vehicles is nearly $70 billion.

The federal government and the states are currently investing $70 million annually, less than 30 cents per capita each year, in research to identify ways of reducing this national public health problem. This level of spending is disproportionate to the size of the problem, the opportunity for reducing loss, and the public investment in research on other major public health problems. The nation is spending roughly 8 times as much on victims of heart disease and nearly 17 times as much on victims of cancer per year of productive work life lost (Figure ES-1).

Highway safety is the shared responsibility of the federal government, state and local governments, and private industry. In their efforts to reduce the loss from motor vehicle crashes, those responsible for highway safety have focused their attention on the three principal elements affecting safety: the human, the vehicle, and the highway environment. NHTSA concentrates its research budget on human- and vehicle-related safety issues (and safety data) and FHWA, on the highway environment. In the private sector, the primary sponsors of research—the automobile manufacturers and suppliers—focus on product design and development to enhance vehicle safety.

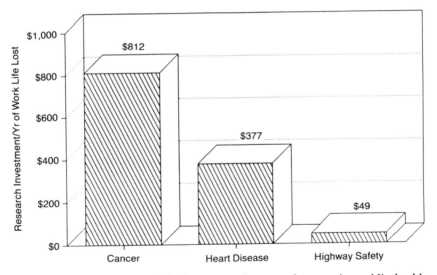

FIGURE ES-1   Annual public investment in research on major public health problems per year of potential work life lost before age 65 for FY1988 (data from National Cancer Institute; National Heart, Lung, and Blood Institute; sources listed in Figure 1-2 and Table 2-2).

During the mid-1960s, a federally funded national program of highway safety research was created to support the new federal regulation of motor vehicle safety and state highway safety program standards. In the decades that followed, research sponsored by both government and industry laid the foundation for many advances in highway safety: introduction of motor vehicle safety features, such as safety belts and energy-absorbing steering columns; design of more forgiving highway barrier systems and roadside hardware that breaks away on impact; enforcement strategies and licensing actions to deter alcohol-impaired driving; and improved emergency medical services to increase postcrash survivability. The research is paying off. Although motor vehicle travel has more than doubled since the mid-1960s, the number of deaths per 100 million vehicle miles traveled has been cut by more than half. Research has contributed to this decline in the death rate by identifying, developing, and evaluating promising safety strategies and interventions, which have guided safety programs and investments.

Today there is reason to doubt whether this rate of progress can be sustained. As motor vehicle travel has been projected to increase, new safety problems loom on the horizon. Although further safety gains can be realized by the application of the knowledge already gained, the capacity to address emerging problems is not being developed. The primary public sponsor of highway safety research, the federal government, has reduced its support for research despite funding of a new program on injury control sponsored by the Centers for Disease Control (CDC). Federal funding averaged about $55 million in inflation-adjusted dollars annually between 1975 and 1981 but declined to an annual average of about $35 million after 1981—a reduction of about 40 percent—where it has remained (Figure ES-2). As resources have been cut, some program areas have been eliminated and the scope of others has narrowed as the agencies have emphasized short-term research in support of specific rulemaking and other agency responsibilities. The major casualty of the cuts has been the capacity to sustain long-term programs of research and to develop new researchers in disciplines such as biomechanics and human factors that are critical to making further advances in injury reduction and crash avoidance. Many of the scientists trained in highway safety have left the field because of the lack of research support.

GAPS IN CURRENT RESEARCH

Progress in highway safety is constrained by the need to rebuild the capacity to undertake long-term programs of research. One consequence of the neglect of this category of research is that the federal government and motor vehicle manufacturers are making large investment decisions with limited knowledge of their safety benefits.

Effects of Research Gaps

Large Implementation Costs

Many safety standards entail substantial implementation costs, so it is essential to know to what extent these investments would save lives and reduce injuries. For example, NHTSA's proposed regulation to improve vehicle occupant protection in side-impact crashes could cost as much as $100 per new car or more than $1 billion annually. Industry is critical of the criteria (and the crash dummy) that NHTSA has proposed for testing injury in side-impact crashes and maintains that the agency has overestimated the safety benefits of the proposed standard. General Motors has offered alternative criteria, but federal funding of research on the biomechanics of injury has not been adequate to support the scientific studies and testing necessary to examine alternative measures and resolve these controversies.

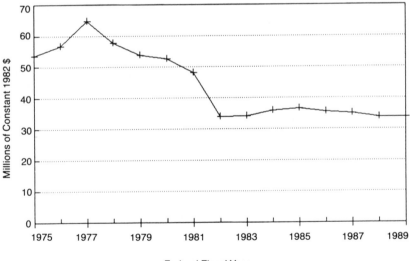

FIGURE ES-2 Federal funding for highway safety research, 1975–1989; figures are deflated using the GNP price deflator as reported in the U.S. Budget (data from Associate Administrator for Research and Development, NHTSA; Office of Fiscal Services and Office of Motor Carriers, FHWA; and Assistant Director for Extramural Research, CDC).

Unknown Safety Benefits

New technologies with the ability to provide drivers with considerably more information on vehicle and highway conditions, such as navigational display systems, are being rapidly developed for passenger cars. The technology could reduce the problem of driver inattention by providing advance warning of risky situations; however, too much information could overload and distract the driver, particularly older drivers, who tend to process information more slowly than younger ones. Human factors research to study the interaction between driver and vehicle is currently inadequate to understand these trade-offs. The design and introduction of these technologies are therefore likely to proceed without the benefit of important data.

Lost Opportunities

Over the next several decades, major portions of the highway system will be rehabilitated or reconstructed as they reach the end of their useful lives, providing a unique opportunity for incorporating safety improvements as part of highway rebuilding projects. However, relatively little is known about the safety consequences of highway design improvements. What little is known is not presented in such a way that highway engineers can readily quantify the associated costs and benefits of alternative improvements. Without a strong case for upgrading design features, highway agencies miss opportunities for safety improvements or make safety improvements that are not cost-effective.

Implications for Safety

The foregoing examples illustrate the potential for making less than fully effective investment decisions and losing opportunities for safety gains when complex decisions are made without an adequate understanding of the consequences. Decision makers find themselves in a dilemma. Should an agency require a safety feature on new cars or a highway design change that may improve safety even though there are insufficient data to demonstrate their effectiveness? Or should safety proposals be postponed until good research has proven their effectiveness? The public is ill served by either approach.

Developing the knowledge that could and should form the basis for these decisions requires sustained funding over many years; the research must be initiated years before the decision process. The investment in research, however, would save many times its costs in avoiding less than fully effective regulations and promoting those safety interventions with a high potential for saving lives and reducing injuries.

RESEARCH AGENDA AND FUNDING REQUIREMENTS

The committee examined future changes in the travel environment and identified six areas (see text box) in which research, if begun now, could help prepare for emerging problems before they become serious.

Even if all of the suggested areas were studied, persistent highway safety problems would likely remain. A well-structured research program must also provide for sustained research on the safety problems of substance-impaired drivers, young drivers, pedestrians, motorcyclists, and bicyclists, which, despite past research and program efforts, continue to contribute a large share of highway fatalities and injuries each year.

Maintaining the current capacity to conduct short-term applied research is also important. Federal agencies need research to address short-term regulatory and programmatic issues. The states, which are more directly responsible for administering safety-related programs, must have the capability to evaluate specific safety interventions.

TOPICS FOR FUTURE RESEARCH

• **Crash Avoidance**   Human error is the major factor contributing to motor vehicle crashes. An expanded program of human factors research could improve understanding of driver attention and work-load capacities, including the performance capabilities and limitations of older drivers, older pedestrians, and commercial drivers, to provide the basis for developing driver licensing and education programs, vehicle design modifications, and highway and traffic design improvements to accommodate these high-risk groups.

• **Occupant Protection**   The continuing trend toward smaller passenger vehicles and larger trucks underscores the importance of further study on ways to increase the use of effective occupant protection devices. Further advances in vehicle crashworthiness and safety design, particularly for more vulnerable older populations, require an expanded program of biomechanics research on the underlying mechanisms of injury and age- and sex-related differences in human tolerance to injury. This research is essential to develop a scientific basis for safety engineering and regulation.

continued on following page

• **Highway Safety Design and Operation** The aging of the highway infrastructure presents an opportunity for making safety improvements to accommodate changes in the driver and vehicle population. More needs to be known about the safety benefits of alternative highway design and traffic engineering improvements to accommodate a wide range of vehicle types, congested highway conditions, and the special problems of an aging population of drivers and pedestrians, and to weigh these against the costs of improvements to determine which improvements can yield net safety benefits and where they are best employed.

• **Postcrash Acute Care and Rehabilitation** Congested highways will make emergency access more difficult, and growing numbers of elderly crash victims are likely to strain acute care and rehabilitation facilities. Examining better methods of providing rapid access to crash victims on congested highways and in rural areas, identifying the special care needs of the elderly, and addressing problems in health care financing for trauma centers should help ensure continued advances in postcrash care.

• **Management of Highway Safety** Better understanding of the capabilities and limitations of elderly and commercial drivers and the constraints of a more congested highway system is likely to require modifications in current licensing programs and enforcement practices. Better methods of screening drivers and tailoring driving privileges to driver capabilities should be devised; more efficient methods of licensing, vehicle inspection, and enforcement should be studied, including the potential for greater use of automated technologies.

• **Driver Information and Vehicle Control Technologies** New driver information and vehicle control systems being developed as part of IVHS have the potential to reduce the risk of collisions by providing drivers with additional information and possibly automating some functions, such as emergency braking. If these benefits are to be realized, more needs to be known about driver responses to a more automated and information-intensive environment, so that the potential for information overload, driver distraction, or driver complacency can be minimized.

Finally, federal agencies must maintain and improve highway safety data bases, which support research as well as the management and monitoring of highway safety programs. These data bases are essential and are most effectively managed and maintained at the national level.

Supporting these activities requires adequate funding and a sustained commitment. Existing funds are already spread thin and cannot accomplish all of these tasks. Additional annual federal funding of $30 million to $40 million (in 1990 dollars), growing 5 to 7 percent annually in real terms as capacity develops over a 5- to 10-year period, is the minimum judged necessary by the committee to provide for short-term research capacity, maintain data-base support, and build long-term research capability.

New funding commitments must be accompanied by changes in the way that research is currently conducted to ensure sustained support for long-term programs of research, encourage research of high quality, and stimulate innovation.

MANAGING RESEARCH TO ENCOURAGE INNOVATION

Effective research programs should nurture and develop researchers in key research disciplines and foster an environment that rewards creativity and excellence. In recent years, the research programs within the primary federal agencies that sponsor highway safety research—NHTSA and FHWA—have not been provided sufficient funding to fully pursue these goals. The reasons are many—declining appropriations for research, changing political priorities of agency administrators, and pressures for rapid response to regulatory and programmatic questions.

Institutional capability to conduct programs of long-term research was an issue of great concern to the committee. Two strategies were examined: (*a*) concentrating additional research funds at NHTSA and FHWA but with important modifications in the way that the funds would be used, and (*b*) spreading the research funds among several organizations to tap the research management skills of other agencies that are perceived to be better insulated from short-term political and programmatic demands.

The majority of the committee concluded that the additional resources would be most effectively spent if they were concentrated in NHTSA and FHWA where highway safety is a mission responsibility. One member would have preferred a pluralistic approach, but even that member concurred with a substantial increase in resources for an expanded program of research at NHTSA and FHWA.

The committee was cognizant of the risks of this strategy—DOT's imperfect track record of supporting quality research and building a corps of scientific researchers as well as the difficulty of conducting long-term research in a political environment. Nevertheless, the current administration of the Department of Transportation is perceived to be committed to creating a climate more conducive to new ideas and new approaches. Additional funds allocated by Congress should reinforce these developments by focusing on the following specific activities.

Restoration of Capacity at NHTSA and FHWA To Conduct Long-Term Highway Safety Research

• Provision of multiyear funding of university centers and other research institutions as well as graduate programs and research fellowships to train new researchers in fields of highway safety.
• Peer review of research proposals and findings; provision for unsolicited research proposals; more flexible funding methods, such as cooperative agreements and grants; and encouragement of small awards to individual researchers—mechanisms that are within the agencies' current authority.
• Improved coordination of research through joint planning of long-term highway safety research agendas by NHTSA, FHWA, and the recently created CDC injury control program; joint programming of research on topics that cross traditional DOT mission agency responsibilities, such as the effects on safety of new technologies and the aging of the population; and preparation of multiyear research plans with input from other appropriate federal agencies, the states, and private industry.

University Research Centers

Biomechanics Research

The federal government should provide multiyear funding to establish one or two university centers of excellence to conduct long-term research in biomechanics; this research is critical to making further advances in injury mitigation and vehicle crashworthiness. Developing a comprehensive research program in biomechanics requires expensive laboratory and testing equipment; concentrating the research in no more than two facilities with state-of-the-art equipment and expanding on existing facilities where possible will ensure that the majority of the funding is used for research.

Research proposals and findings should be peer reviewed to encourage research of high quality; the research facilities should be available to industry, government, and academic researchers alike on a competitive basis; and adequate provision should be made for the education and training of new researchers. This program is essential to developing a scientific basis for motor vehicle regulation.

Crash Avoidance Research

Multiyear funding should also be provided for three to five university centers to support research in human factors and other disciplines related to new technologies and strategies for crash avoidance. The number of centers should be limited to allow each to have adequate funds to support a program of excellent research. Research should be peer reviewed and provision made for education of new researchers. At the level of additional funding recommended in this report, the funds should be used for research and not to support major investment in equipment, such as a national advanced driving simulator.

New Cooperative Program for State-Sponsored Highway Safety Research

In addition to increased research centered at NHTSA and FHWA, the committee recommends a new cooperative program for state-sponsored highway safety research to encourage more state funding and to stimulate joint projects between states on topics of common interest. The primary objectives of the program would be to involve state-level highway safety professionals, such as motor vehicle administrators and law enforcement officials, in proposing research on now relatively neglected driver- and vehicle-related issues; and to encourage pooling of funds on topics of common interest to reduce duplication of effort and maximize the use of limited research dollars. Funds from Section 402 of the Highway Safety Act should be made available to initiate such research if they are matched by state funds. (Research should be defined as an eligible use of federal 402 funds in reauthorizing legislation.) The program could be modeled on the existing National Cooperative Highway Research Program, managed by the American Association of State Highway and Transportation Officials in cooperation with DOT and the National Academy of Sciences, which pools funds for joint state research on highway-related issues.

BENEFITS OF AN EXPANDED HIGHWAY SAFETY RESEARCH PROGRAM

Recommended changes in the scale and direction of research activities, if targeted well, should provide a level of effort more commensurate with the size of the highway safety problem. The additional $30 million to $40 million in federal funding required to support these changes represents about a 50 percent increase over the current annual spending on highway safety research from combined federal and state sources of approximately $70 million. Nevertheless, even if current spending were doubled, highway safety research would still be underfunded relative to other major public health problems and the number of lives lost in traffic crashes. Moreover, the benefits of an expanded highway safety research effort would extend beyond lives saved. Motor vehicle crashes result in permanently disabling head and spinal cord injuries, expensive medical care, and costly property damage that could also be averted.

Although it is not possible to quantify them precisely, the benefits of an expanded research program are almost certain to outweigh the costs. Unlike many other public health problems, where a single breakthrough like development of a vaccine can achieve a major savings in lives, further advances in highway safety are likely to come from incremental improvements through a wide range of safety interventions. Research plays an integral role in identifying those interventions with the greatest potential for real gains and, perhaps equally important, in avoiding large investments in less than fully effective safety regulations and programs. For these reasons, the committee strongly recommends a new federal and state commitment to an expanded highway safety research program.

Traffic deaths and injuries cost the nation tens of billions of dollars each year and untold pain and suffering. Sustained investment in research is needed to provide the knowledge to make further progress in addressing this major public health problem. Yet, at a time when new highway safety problems are emerging and spending on safety must compete with other societal goals, the knowledge base has not kept pace; research budgets have been cut, research programs narrowed in focus, and researchers have left the field. Failure to invest adequately in research increases the risk that future expenditures on safety programs and regulations will not be made wisely. A renewed commitment to long-term programs of research is critical to lay the foundations for judicious investment decisions and to realize the full potential for saving lives and dollars.

1

Overview of the Highway Safety Problem

Motor vehicle crashes are a leading cause of death and injury in the United States. During the 1980s, 40,000 to 50,000 lives were lost each year on the nation's highways and nearly 80 times that number were injured annually. Even without quantification of the pain and suffering endured from these crashes, the drain on society's resources is enormous: $40 billion (in 1986 dollars) in lost wages and medical costs and an additional $30 billion in property damage each year.

Today's highway safety record, although it represents a heavy toll in annual deaths, injuries, and property damage, represents an improvement over the past. The absolute number of fatalities was only slightly lower in the 1980s than in the 1960s, but vehicle travel doubled during this period, resulting in a decline in the death rate measured in fatalities per 100 million vehicle miles traveled from 5.1 in 1960 to 2.3 in 1988 (NHTSA 1989, 1–6). Annual fatalities per capita, however, remained relatively constant at about 2 fatalities per 10,000 persons (NHTSA 1989, 1–6).

There is reason to doubt whether past improvements can be sustained. Continued growth in motor vehicle travel and expected changes in the travel environment—increasing numbers of older drivers and pedestrians, growth in large-truck travel, and aging highway infrastructure—have the potential to slow, if not reverse, the progress of the past several decades.

Research can provide the knowledge to tackle emerging safety problems. Building the knowledge base, however, requires a sustained effort by researchers from a wide range of disciplines operating in an environment conducive to innovation. Moreover, research is only a first step. Safety gains are achieved once ideas have been put into practice—a process that is often lengthy and costly. Unfortunately, cutbacks in federal funding for highway safety research in the 1980s have diminished the capacity to take even this first step. As funds have been reduced, the time horizon of many research programs has become increasingly short term,

13

and the training of new researchers has languished. What research funds are available have not always been used effectively, hampered by research agendas that are often narrowly defined and contracting methods that limit researchers' scope of inquiry.

SCOPE OF STUDY AND ORGANIZATION OF REPORT

If research is to play a vital role in addressing the highway safety problems of the next several decades, the scope and direction of current research programs must be reevaluated. The Federal Highway Administration (FHWA) and the National Highway Traffic Safety Administration (NHTSA) jointly funded the Strategic Transportation Research Study (STRS) for Highway Safety to undertake this critical assessment.

Highway safety research is currently targeted at the three principal elements affecting highway safety: the human, the vehicle, and the environment. Public agencies responsible for research have divided these areas among them: NHTSA concentrates its research budget on human- and vehicle-related safety issues (and data) and FHWA, on the highway environment. In the private sector, the primary sponsors of research—the automobile manufacturers and suppliers—conduct research on design and engineering improvements to enhance vehicle safety.

This historical division of responsibilities limits opportunities for comprehensive assessment of issues that cut across traditional lines. For example, limited research has been conducted on such crosscutting issues as the effect of intelligent vehicle-highway system (IVHS) technologies on driver performance or the effect of changing demographics on vehicle and highway design.

The STRS for Highway Safety took a broad systems perspective and attempted to identify how research could be restructured to focus better on emerging as well as persistent highway safety problems. The study committee was particularly interested in how the research process could be better managed to encourage innovation and more effective use of resources. Specifically, the study committee

- Reviewed the characteristics and scale of existing highway safety problems and research,
- Identified promising areas for research that merit more attention or that warrant continuing study, and
- Examined the financial and institutional arrangements that may be needed to refocus research on these priorities.

In short, the committee took a fresh look at the direction, funding levels, and management of highway safety research.

The timing of this effort could not be better. The recently released National Transportation Policy of the U.S. Department of Transportation (DOT) identified safety as the top priority of the department (DOT 1990, 7). The current administration proposes to devote additional resources to research and development in general and to highway safety in particular. Congress has the opportunity to fund these proposals in the upcoming reauthorization of the federal surface transportation assistance program in 1991 (DOT 1990, 118) and the annual reauthorization of the National Traffic and Motor Vehicle Safety Act. This study should help identify more precisely where research funds are likely to yield the biggest safety dividends.

Congressional support for highway safety measures is building as the costs of injuries in motor vehicle crashes become better defined. For example, legislation to encourage states to enact mandatory helmet and safety belt use laws is being proposed to reduce rising medical costs that are passed on to society from injuries in motor vehicle crashes and to stem the loss of productive citizens.[1]

To set the context for the subsequent critical review of highway safety research, a review of the magnitude of the highway safety problem and expected changes in system characteristics that are likely to affect the safety of motor vehicle travel in the future takes up the remainder of this chapter. In Chapter 2, the role and contribution of research to highway safety are examined, and the trends in research priorities and funding of the past 20 years are reviewed, on the basis of which critical gaps in current research programs are identified. Promising areas for research to address emerging safety problems are described in Chapter 3, and persistent safety problems are discussed in Chapter 4. Chapter 5 examines needed changes in the way that highway safety research is structured and Chapter 6, in the funding of research, to ensure that recommended changes in the direction of research can be sustained.

DIMENSIONS OF THE HIGHWAY SAFETY PROBLEM

Although few would deny that enhancing safety is a laudable goal, measures to improve highway safety compete with other legitimate societal goals, such as meeting the mobility needs of the elderly, or increasing support for the war on drugs, or supporting safety programs in another transportation mode. Making a strong case for highway safety requires a consensus on the size and seriousness of the problem.

Yet millions of Americans drive each day and complete their trips safely, thus reinforcing the individual's perception that the risks involved in driving are low. Motor vehicle crashes and their consequences are large in the aggregate—nearly 18 million crashes, 4 million injuries, and about 45,000 fatalities each year (NHTSA 1988b, x), but the risk of a crash is low on average. With about 160 million drivers, each driving an average of 11,500 mi per year, the occurrence of a crash, on average, is one every 102,000 driver miles or nearly every 9 driver years. The occurrence of a fatality is considerably less—one every 41 million driver miles or 3,600 driver years. Moreover, most motor vehicle crashes (with the exception of bus crashes), when they do occur, typically involve relatively few persons and thus do not attract the same public attention as airplane or train crashes.

Yet averages do not tell the full story. The condition of the driver and the type of vehicle can change the risk equation dramatically. For example, a young, unbelted, intoxicated driver in a small vehicle has a 1,000 times greater risk of being killed on an Interstate highway than a middle-aged, belted, alcohol-free driver in a heavier car (Evans et al. 1990, 243).

When viewed as a public health problem, motor vehicle crashes are a national problem of the magnitude of cancer and heart disease.

Crash Incidence and Consequences

Motor vehicle crashes are the leading cause of injuries in the United States (NRC 1985, 21) and rank sixth as a cause of death (Census Bureau 1989, 78). In 1986, the latest year for which data on all motor vehicle crashes are available, the National Accident Sampling System (NASS) reported 17.7 million crashes (NHTSA 1988b, x). Of this total, 2.8 million were identified as injury crashes, which resulted in more than 46,000 fatalities and 3.9 million injuries in that year (see text box). Crash survivors were hospitalized for a total of 2.2 million days and lost 14.6 million days of work in 1986 alone (NHTSA 1988b, x). The remaining 14.9 million crashes generally involved property damage and minor injuries.

Motor vehicle crashes are of particular concern because they involve the young. They are the largest single cause of death by a wide margin for those between the ages of 1 and 24 and are second only to cancer for those between the ages of 25 and 44 (Figure 1-1). Although many more people die each year from heart disease and cancer than from motor vehicle crashes, when deaths are viewed from the perspective of potential years of work life lost before age 65,[2] motor vehicle crashes are nearly as serious a problem as cancer and heart disease (Figure 1-2).

Injury crashes		2,801,000
Fatalities	46,056	
Injuries		
Severe (MAIS ≥ 3)	161,973	
Moderate (MAIS < 3)	3,827,337	
Total	3,989,310	
Property damage crashes		
Police-reported		3,589,000
Reported to all other sources		11,310,000
Subtotal		14,899,000
Total motor vehicle crashes		17,700,000

NOTE: MAIS = Maximum Abbreviated Injury Scale; MAIS < 3 includes minor and moderate injuries; MAIS ≥ 3 includes serious, severe, and critical injuries (NHTSA 1988b, 47).

SOURCE: for fatalities, NASS (NHTSA 1988b, x); for injuries by MAIS, special computer tabulation from NHTSA.

Recent interest in injury as a public health problem (NRC 1985) has focused attention on the contribution of motor vehicle crashes to injury. (The main causes of injury, in addition to traffic crashes, are falls, firearms, poisonings, fires and burns, drownings, and near drownings.) Motor vehicle crashes are the leading cause of injury death, accounting for one-third of all fatal injuries (Rice et al. 1989, xx), and the second leading

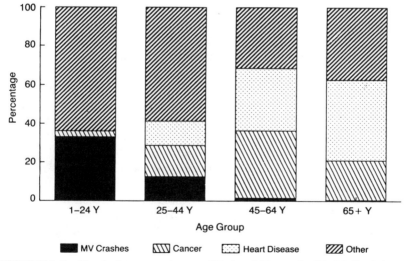

FIGURE 1-1   Deaths by age and cause (National Center for Health Statistics 1987, 246–305).

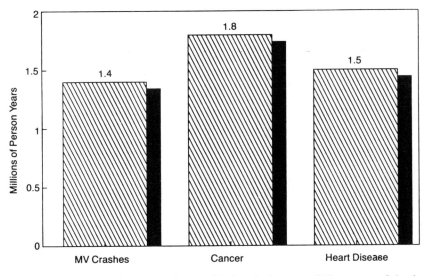

FIGURE 1-2   Potential years of work life lost before age 65 by cause of death (Centers for Disease Control 1990, 21; NHTSA 1989, 1–27)

cause of nonfatal injury; they accounted for 22 percent of hospitalized and 9 percent of nonhospitalized injured persons (Rice et al. 1989, xxi, xxvii).[3] They are also the cause of many long-term disabling injuries, such as those to the spinal cord and brain (Rice et al. 1989, 17).

Crash Costs

Motor vehicle crashes impose a substantial burden on society. In 1986 the monetary costs of motor vehicle crashes reached $70 billion (Table 1-1).[4] These costs cover two categories: crashes reported to the police, for which NHTSA collects detailed data, and crashes reported to all other sources (e.g., insurance companies, motor vehicle authorities), which are typically more numerous than police-reported crashes but generally not as serious. Detailed information is not available about the second category.

The costs reported here include property damage to vehicles; medical costs; losses in household and workplace productivity; police, fire, and ambulance services; legal and court costs; and overhead costs of insurance and public welfare (Miller et al. 1989, 304). They do not include delays from crashes, which can represent a substantial cost by reducing the flow of movement and goods on the highways.[5] Moreover, there is no attempt to place a value on the social loss from early deaths or on the pain and suffering resulting from injuries caused by motor vehicle crashes.

TABLE 1-1 MOTOR VEHICLE CRASH COSTS, 1986 (NHTSA 1988a, x; Miller et al. 1989, 305, 311; Miller 1989, A-1)

Crash Statistic	Crash Incidence	Crash Consequences	Total Cost[a] ($ billions)	Percent of Total Cost
Crashes Reported to Police				
No. of injury crashes	2,801,000			
Fatalities		46,056	19.6	40.2
Injuries				
Severe (MAIS ≥ 3)		161,973	9.5	19.5
Moderate (MAIS < 3)		3,827,337	13.0	26.6
No. of crashes with property damage and minor injury	3,589,000		6.7	13.7
			48.8	100.0
Crashes Reported to All Other Sources				
No. of crashes with property damage and minor injury	11,310,000		21.2	
Total no. of crashes	17,700,000		70.0	

[a] These costs (in 1986 dollars) are monetary costs only. The total investment to avoid death and injury valued by the "willingness-to-pay" method (see text) would be $184 billion in 1986 dollars.

An analysis of crash costs by consequence for the better-documented police-reported crashes shows that injuries are the single largest cost category (more than 45 percent of total police-reported monetary crash costs) (Table 1-1). The high cost of injuries reflects the lost earning potential and costly medical care of those with severe injuries. For particularly severe injuries, such as those to the brain and spinal cord, these costs can be far more substantial than the cost of a fatality.[6] Injury costs vary widely, however, depending on injury severity. Severe injuries, that is, those rated 3 or higher on the Maximum Abbreviated Injury Scale (MAIS) used by NHTSA, account for only 4 percent of the total number of crash injuries, but represent 42 percent of the total monetary cost of injury.

Fatalities also represent a major share (40 percent) of total police-reported monetary crash costs (Table 1-1), reflecting substantial productivity losses of the young, who are overrepresented in motor vehicle crashes. Together, injuries and fatalities represent more than four-fifths of total police-reported monetary crash costs. Property damage accounts for the remainder. Total property damage costs are substantial, particularly if crashes that are not reported to the police are included (Table 1-1). However, property damage costs per crash are small relative to the monetary cost of an injury or a fatality.

The total monetary costs of motor vehicle crashes—$70 billion in 1986 dollars—are comparable with the monetary costs of cancer and heart disease, the two leading causes of death in the United States, although the latter result in 10 to 16 times more fatalities, respectively, than motor vehicle crashes (Census Bureau 1989, 78). The monetary costs of heart disease were estimated at $78.6 billion (in 1986 dollars) by the American Heart Association (AHA 1987) and the monetary costs of cancer at $71.5 billion (in 1985 dollars) by the National Center for Health Statistics (ACS 1987, 25).

Monetary costs do not include any estimate of the pain and suffering and loss in quality of life associated with injury and death in motor vehicle crashes. If these were valued by the "willingness-to-pay" method, which reflects what individuals are willing to pay to prevent an injury or fatality and the related costs that society saves, the amount that the public would be willing to pay to avoid these crashes was $184 billion in 1986 dollars (Table 1-1) (Miller et al. 1989, 311).[7]

Historical Trends in Motor Vehicle Crashes

Considerable progress has been made in reducing death and injury on the highways over the past several decades.

Fatality Rates per Vehicle Mile

Although motor vehicle fatalities have grown by nearly 50 percent in the four decades since the end of World War II, the amount of vehicle travel has grown even faster, resulting in an overall reduction in fatality rates, measured as deaths per 100 million vehicle miles of travel (VMT) (Figure 1-3).[8] The exception is a brief period during the early to mid-1960s when fatalities climbed to more than 50,000 and fatality rates rose also, reversing a long downward trend. Alarm about this reversal, spearheaded by a series of highly publicized congressional hearings on automotive safety (e.g., Senator Ribicoff's subcommittee of the Senate Government Operations Committee), helped build support for the first federal regulation of motor vehicle safety (Flink 1975).

The decline in fatality rates reflects a combination of improvements to the vehicle and the highway as well as changing demographics and underlying social norms. Some of these factors are discussed briefly here.

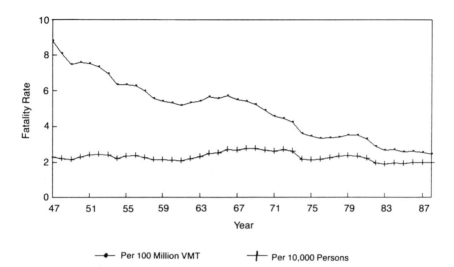

FIGURE 1-3   Motor vehicle fatality rates per vehicle miles of travel (VMT) versus motor vehicle fatality rates per capita, 1947–1987 (*Accident Facts* 1989, 70–71).

The National Traffic and Motor Vehicle Safety Act and the Highway Safety Act of 1966 authorized the first federal motor vehicle and highway safety regulations. The initial federal safety standards for new passenger vehicles became effective in January 1968 (Crandall et al. 1986, 47), resulting in design features that improved vehicle crashworthiness and crash avoidance. Head restraints, energy-absorbing steering columns, penetration-resistant windshields, dual braking systems, improved door-locking systems, and safety belts all became standard equipment on passenger cars.

During the past three decades, construction of the Interstate highway system has been essentially completed and the share of miles driven on the safer, limited-access Interstate highway system has grown rapidly. In 1961 only 7 percent of all travel was on Interstate highways (Crandall et al. 1986, 46); by 1989 the share had risen to 22 percent of all travel (FHWA 1989, 173).

The urbanization of America also contributed to safer travel. Rural travel typically is characterized by higher fatalities and fatality rates than urban travel, in part because of higher speeds on less-congested rural roads. The share of travel on urban roads grew from more than two-fifths of total travel in the early 1960s to three-fifths today, contributing to the reduction in fatality rates (FHWA 1985, 226; FHWA 1989, 173). This effect is offset to some degree by the greater number of injuries and higher injury rates from multiple-vehicle crashes on congested urban highways.[9]

These injuries, however, tend to be less severe than those on rural highways.[10]

In 1973 imposition of the 55-mph speed limit accompanied by fuel shortages brought about another decline in highway fatality rates. Although the main purpose of speed regulations was energy conservation, fatality rates dropped sharply as average speed declined and drivers drove at more uniform speeds (Figure 1-3).

During the 1970s, improvements in emergency medical services and response times as well as the development of trauma care centers helped to avert fatalities through more timely and effective medical care.

In the late 1970s and 1980s, measures directed toward both the driver and the vehicle are credited with continued reductions in fatality rates. Renewed attention to reduction of alcohol-impaired driving and declining alcohol consumption (Crandall et al. 1986, 46; *The Liquor Handbook* 1988, 223) reduced the incidence of alcohol-related motor vehicle fatalities. State laws raising the drinking age to 21 and a decline in the number of drivers under 25 (Crandall et al. 1986, 46; *Accident Facts* 1989, 54) also reduced the number of fatalities among high-risk young drivers. Finally, the dramatic increase in the number of states with mandatory safety belt use laws has resulted in reductions in fatalities and injuries attributable to the known effectiveness of occupant restraints. In 1984 only one state, New York, had passed a safety belt law; by 1990, 36 states and the District of Columbia had enacted such legislation (NHTSA 1990a), but safety belt use is still far from universal (NHTSA 1989, 2–19).

Some researchers have also attributed the decline in motor vehicle fatality rates to the general evolution of motorized travel in all countries (Haight 1984, 137; Evans 1989, 7). Indeed, a comparison of U.S. fatality rates with those of other developed countries from 1970 to the most recent year for which data are available shows a similar pattern of long-term decline (Figure 1-4). The United States, however, has the distinction of having the lowest fatality rate.

Fatality Rates per Capita

The common method used to analyze hazard in the field of public health is to look at fatality rates per capita. When motor vehicle fatality rates are measured in this way, the picture that emerges is quite different (Figure 1-3). Instead of declining, fatality rates appear as a nearly horizontal line. Thus, although travel for a specific distance (i.e., fatality rates measured per 100 million VMT) has become safer, the risk to the affected population (i.e., fatality rates measured per 1 million persons) has remained

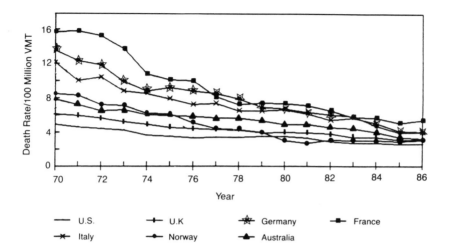

FIGURE 1-4   Motor vehicle fatality rates for selected countries, 1970–1986 (MVMA 1989, 92; MVMA 1987, 92; MVMA 1982, 92; MVMA 1977, 56).

relatively constant. Haight explains the latter phenomenon as a function of the dramatic rise in vehicle travel over this period, which has increased vehicle occupant and pedestrian exposure to crashes (Haight 1984, 138).

Fatalities and Injuries by Road User Group

Aggregate figures on fatalities and injuries and fatality and injury rates obscure differences among specific road user groups. Not surprisingly, passenger car occupants account for the majority of traffic fatalities and injuries—54 percent and 73 percent, respectively (Table 1-2). (These data are for 1986, the latest year for which injury and fatality data are available.) Occupants of trucks and motorcycles, as well as pedestrians, experience large numbers of fatalities and injuries on the highway (Table 1-2). Together, they account for 40 percent of all fatalities and nearly a quarter of all injuries.

When mileage-based fatality and injury rates are calculated for those user groups for which exposure data are available, large differences are evident. Motorcycle drivers and riders have the highest fatality and injury rates per 100 million VMT of any user group by a large margin (Table 1-2). However, these comparisons should be made with care. Truck occupant fatality and injury rates are lower than those of some other road users, but this in part reflects the fact that in truck-involved crashes, it is usually the occupants of the other vehicle that are killed or injured.

TABLE 1-2   FATALITIES, INJURIES, AND RATES BY ROAD USER
GROUP

Road User Group	Fatalities	Fatality[a] Rate	Injuries	Injury[a] Rate
Vehicle occupants				
Passenger cars	24,922	1.9	2,895,272	222.5
Trucks	7,307	1.4	633,431	122.0
Buses	38	0.7	14,344	282.7
Motorcycles	4,551	48.4	171,945	1,829.8
Other	1,393	N.A.	53,709	N.A.
Nonoccupants				
Pedestrians	6,771	N.A.	125,920	N.A.
Pedalcyclists	941	N.A.	82,796	N.A.
Other	133	N.A.	11,893	N.A.
Total	46,056	2.5	3,989,310	217.4

NOTE: N.A. = not available. Exposure data on a mileage basis are not available for these user groups.
[a]Measured per 100 million vehicle miles traveled.
SOURCE: for fatalities, FARS (NHTSA 1988a, 6-2, 8-2, 8-9); for injuries, special computer tabulation from NHTSA; for mileage data, *Highway Statistics* (FHWA 1988b, 171).

Linking Fatalities and Injuries

One consequence of the general trend toward improved survivability in crashes is increased incidence of injury. In the United States, data on motor vehicle injuries have been available only since 1979 and are based on a sample from which national figures are estimated. The figures for 1979–1986 show some evidence of increasing injuries relative to fatalities. In 1979–1980 there were 67 injuries for every motor vehicle fatality (NHTSA 1984); by 1986 the number had risen to 85 to 1, a more than 25 percent increase (NHTSA 1988b). Canadian data for a much longer period—1965 to 1985—show a doubling in the ratio of injuries to fatalities (Hauer 1988, 3). Further monitoring of these trends and more detailed analysis of changes in injury severity patterns are warranted in view of the potentially important implications of increased injuries for the nation's medical care system.

LOOKING TO THE FUTURE

Can improvements in the nation's safety record be sustained or bettered in the future? For the past several decades, the pace of safety improvements has offset increases in motor vehicle travel, bringing steady reductions in fatality rates measured as deaths per 100 million VMT (Figure 1-3). In recent years, however, the slope of the curve has flattened, suggesting that the decline in fatality rates may be progressing more slowly than in the past.

Projecting Fatality Rates

Motor vehicle fatalities ranged between 40,000 and 50,000 annually during the 1980s (NHTSA 1989, 1–6). To keep fatalities below 50,000 by the year 2005, fatality rates would have to drop from 2.3 deaths per 100 million VMT in 1988[11] to 1.45 to 1.75 deaths per 100 million VMT by 2005, a reduction of between one-fourth and one-third. These projections assume a slowing in the annual growth rate of travel from the 3.5 percent average of the last two decades to between 2 and 3 percent over the next decade and a half (U.S. Congress 1989, IV-5).

Part of this reduction could be achieved by further implementing the safety measures that are known to be effective in reducing motor vehicle fatalities and injuries. For example, if passenger vehicle occupants could be convinced to buckle up so that safety belt usage would increase from the current 45 percent to 70 percent by 2005 (NHTSA 1989, 2–17), fatalities would be reduced by nearly 13 percent and fatality rates would drop to 2 deaths per 100 million VMT, assuming the highest travel projections.[12]

Expected Changes in Travel Environment

Further gains may be achieved by addressing emerging safety problems. Identifiable problems are on the horizon that can be redressed if research begins now. Changes in the travel environment of the next several decades—an older driver and pedestrian population, more large-truck traffic, increasing disparity in vehicle size and weight, growing congestion, an aging infrastructure, and new vehicle and highway technologies—are all likely to have a significant effect on the rate of highway safety gains. Each of these topics and its implications for travel safety are discussed in the following subsections.

Demographic Changes

The aging of the population will affect both ends of the age distribution, with differing effects on highway safety.

Older Drivers and Pedestrians

The growing population of elderly drivers and pedestrians is likely to result in more traffic fatalities and injuries. Older drivers typically experience reduced driving skills because of the degradation of functional and cognitive skills that accompanies aging (TRB 1988, 72). With age, vision, especially night vision, degrades and reflexes slow, so that older drivers generally have slower decision-reaction times. To compensate for these changes, many older drivers restrict their night driving. They also tend to drive more slowly than prevailing conditions, which, somewhat paradoxically, may increase their risk of crash involvement; uniform speeds are best for traffic flow and safety (Hauer 1971). When crashes occur, older persons are more likely to be injured because of their physical vulnerability (Mackay 1988).

The increased crash and injury risk of the elderly is evident in the crash statistics. Older drivers (i.e., those 65 years and older) have the highest crash rates of all drivers except those under 25 (Figure 1-5).[13] Drivers aged 75 or over are about two to three times more likely to be involved in a crash (on a mileage-driven basis) than middle-aged drivers.

As the population ages in the coming decades, the number of older vehicle occupants killed in crashes is likely to increase. Currently, about 4,000 older drivers and passengers are killed in motor vehicle crashes each year (Figure 1-6). The aging of the population is expected to reach its peak by 2030, when about 22 percent of the population will be 65 and over (compared with roughly 12 percent currently).

To illustrate the effect of this increase in the elderly population, the most recent occupant death rates were applied to the projected population and age distribution for 2030 (Figure 1-6). Older-occupant deaths could more than double simply because the number of elderly is expected to more than double.

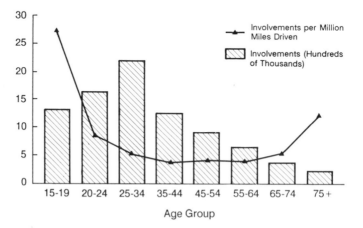

FIGURE 1-5 Driver involvement in traffic crashes and involvement rates by age (TRB 1988, 40).

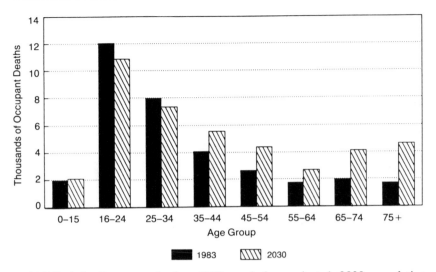

FIGURE 1-6 Occupant deaths, 1983, and for projected 2030 population (NHTSA special computer tabulation and Census Bureau 1984).

Nonoccupant deaths (which are mostly pedestrians but include cyclists) show a different pattern. The death rate (per 100,000 persons) ranges between 2.5 and 3.8 up to age 75; then it increases to roughly 7.4 (NHTSA special computer tabulation; Census Bureau 1984). Because of the sharp increase in pedestrian fatality rates after age 75, the effect of the aging of the population is likely to be much more pronounced on the number and distribution of nonoccupant than on occupant fatalities (Figure 1-7).

Young Drivers and Pedestrians

In contrast to older drivers, the young typically have the best visual ability and reaction times, but often display poor judgment. Young men, in particular, are much more likely than other drivers to drive while impaired by alcohol or other drugs, to speed, to fail to wear safety belts, and to be involved in higher-speed, single-vehicle crashes (Peck 1985; Jonah 1986; TRB 1989). Studies suggest, however, that as more young women are out on their own at fairly young ages, an increasing number are engaging in similar behaviors (*Highway Safety Directions* 1990).

The aging of the population should have a beneficial effect on safety by reducing the share of drivers in the highest-risk youth groups (i.e., ages 15 to 24) (Figure 1-5). However, the absolute number of vehicle occupant deaths will remain highest in these groups (Figure 1-6). Although older

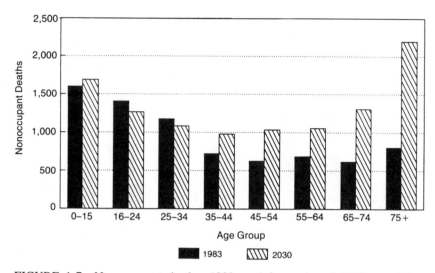

FIGURE 1-7   Nonoccupant deaths, 1983, and for projected 2030 population (NHTSA special computer tabulation and Census Bureau 1984).

pedestrians (i.e., those 65 years and older) are likely to experience the greatest number of fatalities of all age groups, young pedestrians and bicyclists will continue to experience a substantial number of deaths in the decades to come (Figure 1-7).

Changes in Vehicle Mix and Density

During the next several decades, vehicle use patterns are likely to result in an even greater disparity in vehicle sizes and weights on the highway than today, and increasingly congested driving conditions.

Vehicle Mix

Although highways are designed to handle a mix of vehicle types, it is known that crash risk increases with variances in the traffic stream that are introduced because of differences in vehicle performance characteristics, such as speed (Solomon 1964; Cirillo 1968; Hauer 1971). For example, because of their poorer accelerating and braking capabilities, large trucks often operate at lower speeds than the prevailing traffic, particularly on steep grades and in heavy traffic; wide variations in vehicle speeds increase the probability of crashes. Differences in vehicle weight also affect the relative protection afforded vehicle occupants in the event of a crash. Bicyclists and motorcyclists are the most exposed in a crash with a motor vehicle, but in fatal crashes in which a large truck is involved, occupants of the other vehicles account for approximately three-fourths of the fatalities (NHTSA 1989, 6–32).

The disparity in vehicle size and weight is likely to grow during the next several decades. Forecasters at FHWA are predicting a 3.3 percent average annual growth rate for large-truck[14] travel (Highway Performance Monitoring System data base, special computer run), substantially in excess of the 2.34 percent average annual growth rate projected for all vehicle types (U.S. Congress 1989, 90).

The number of light trucks (i.e., those less than 10,000 lb) on the highways has also been growing rapidly as these vehicles are increasingly being used for personal travel. Light trucks now represent nearly one-third of new-vehicle retail sales in the United States (MVMA 1989, 16, 19). Although the weight and size differential between light trucks and passenger vehicles is not as substantial as that between large trucks and passenger vehicles, the passenger vehicle occupant is still likely to be more vulnerable in a crash with a light truck than a crash with another passenger vehicle (NHTSA 1989, 6–10).[15] The occupants of light trucks are also at somewhat greater risk because many of the standard safety features that are, or will soon be, available on passenger cars are not yet required on light trucks. Although NHTSA is in process of extending these standards to light trucks,[16] their benefits will not be fully realized until the current fleet fully turns over, a process requiring 10 to 15 years.

Passenger vehicles are likely to remain small for the foreseeable future because of continuing environmental and energy concerns. Currently, nearly 30 percent of all new-car retail sales, not counting imports, are classified as compacts and subcompacts (MVMA 1990, 15). A recent study by NHTSA (Partyka 1989, 47) found that fatalities (per 100,000 registered cars) were approximately 2.5 to 3 times greater for compacts and subcompacts, respectively, than for full size cars. The higher fatality rate for smaller cars was attributed to their greater vulnerability in multiple-vehicle crashes, which usually involve larger vehicles, and their more frequent involvement in rollover crashes (Partyka 1989, 47).

More bicyclists are also likely to be seen on the highways, increasing the exposure of this highly vulnerable population. Bicycle shipments have grown by more than 40 percent since 1980 (Census Bureau 1989, 227).

Congestion

Vehicles will be traveling on increasingly congested highways, particularly in urban areas at peak hours. The most recent highway needs study

(U.S. Congress 1989, 99) identified new capacity requirements of between 11,250 and 25,000 additional lane miles by 2005, mainly in urban areas, to maintain 1985 system performance levels, but these are unlikely to be built because of right-of-way restrictions and costs. With vehicle travel expected to increase by approximately 50 percent between 1987 and 2005 (U.S. Congress 1989, 90) and the prospects for adding substantial new highway capacity limited, existing highways will be more heavily traveled than they are today.

The implications of increased congestion for safety are not fully understood (Hall and Pendleton 1990). The potential for vehicle conflicts and for multiple-vehicle collisions is heightened with increasing traffic volumes (Hall and Pendleton 1990, 15). However, when crashes do occur, particularly on very congested highways, crash severity may be less than on highways with lower traffic volumes because of lower vehicle speeds. The latter effect appears to be borne out in the data on fatality and injury rates for urban and rural areas discussed earlier.

Aging of the Highway Infrastructure

As the Interstate highway construction program draws to a close with the upcoming reauthorization of the federal highway program in 1991, the emphasis on repair and upgrading of the existing highway system is likely to become an even greater priority than it is today. Major portions of the existing highway network will require rehabilitation and reconstruction as they reach the end of their design lives over the next several decades. Approximately 30 percent of all federal-aid highway funds are already directed toward reconstruction, resurfacing, restoration, and rehabilitation (FHWA 1989, 81–83).

Drivers are likely to be sharing the highways with more work crews, increasing the potential for crashes in construction work zones. Fatalities in work-zone areas are currently about 700 annually (FHWA 1988a, 1). Despite the potential for increased fatalities, rehabilitation of the highway network during the next several decades provides a unique opportunity to improve highway safety by incorporating geometric design and traffic engineering improvements into highway rebuilding projects.

Technological Innovations

New technologies associated with IVHS are emerging with the potential to alter the driving task significantly. Advances in technology will soon provide the driver with substantially more information than in the past. For example, changeable-message signs will provide real-time information about highway conditions, and in-vehicle information devices will provide instant advisories about crashes and congestion as well as navigational information. Vehicles may be equipped with electronic devices to detect and warn the driver of unsafe vehicle conditions (e.g., presence of objects in driver blind spots, impending rollover), unsafe proximity to other vehicles (e.g., radar collision avoidance systems), as well as unsafe driver conditions (e.g., impairment and fatigue). By alerting the driver to impending dangerous situations in time for him to take corrective action, these advanced driver information systems could reduce the risk of crashes. However, these new technologies may prove to be a double-edged sword. Poorly designed systems may overload driver capacity to accept and process the additional information without distraction and actually result in a safety decrement. Overload could be a particular problem for older drivers, who generally process information more slowly than younger drivers (Staplin et al. 1987, 85; TRB 1988, 59).

New technology will also provide drivers with advanced systems of vehicle warning and control. These could range from smart cruise control, which would automatically warn the driver or slow the vehicle when the headway between vehicles narrows to a predetermined interval, to radar braking systems, which would automatically warn the driver to brake or actually control certain braking maneuvers. Again, however, it is unclear how drivers would respond—how they would adjust their driving behavior and perception of risk—if vehicles were equipped with these advanced control systems. Unfortunately, technology appears to be advancing faster than the knowledge of how humans will adapt to it.

CONCLUSION

Currently, about 45,000 lives are lost each year in highway traffic crashes. Traffic fatalities measured per 100 million VMT were 2.3 in 1988, substantially down from their peak of 5.5 in the mid-1960s (NHTSA 1989, 1-6). Among the reasons for this decline are improvements in vehicle design and occupant protection, which have reduced the probability of crashes and lessened the opportunity for injury in crashes; the construction of and increasing travel on the safer limited-access Interstate highway system; implementation and enforcement of measures to reduce alcohol-impaired driving; and improvements in emergency medical services and response times and development of regionalized trauma care centers, which have mitigated the consequences of traffic crashes.

Over the next several decades, the highway environment will continue to change in ways that affect safety. On the positive side, a larger share of the vehicular fleet will have improved safety features and a reduced share of the highest-risk youth groups (i.e., ages 15 to 24) will be driving. On the negative side, travel and congestion will increase, the number of older drivers and pedestrians will rise, cars will become smaller while trucks become larger, and more miles of highway will pose hazards while they are being reconstructed.

The net effect of these changes on safety is not easy to predict. Is the knowledge base sufficiently advanced to begin to tackle these changes before they emerge as major safety problems? This question is addressed in the next chapter.

NOTES

1. The National Traffic Fatality and Injury Reduction Act of 1989 (S. 1007) was introduced by Senator John Chafee, and the National Highway Fatality and Injury Reduction Act of 1990 (H.R. 3925) was introduced by Representative Jim Cooper.
2. "Early deaths" or "years of productive life lost" are commonly used statistics in the public health field to measure the burden of disease on society (Hatziandreu et al. 1988). Many researchers believe that these are better measures of the burden of injury or disease than total deaths, because early deaths place larger burdens on individuals, families, and society than do late deaths.
3. The total estimate of fatal and nonfatal injuries from motor vehicle crashes in 1985 by Rice et al. (xxvii)—5.4 million—is nearly 60 percent higher than that derived from the NASS file for the same year of 3.4 million (NHTSA 1988b, x). The discrepancies reflect the use of different data sources and the lack of uniform coding of injury by cause, which limit the ability of researchers to make accurate estimates of injury incidence.
4. The following costs were assumed: $425,406 per fatality, $2,860 per Maximum Abbreviated Injury Scale (MAIS) 1 injury, $8,058 per MAIS 2 injury, $19,489 per MAIS 3 injury, $155,832 per MAIS 4 injury, $391,314 per MAIS 5 injury (Miller et al. 1989, 305), and $1,875 per property-damage-only (PDO) crash (Miller 1989, A-1). All costs are in 1986 dollars and are applied to 1986 fatalities reported by the Fatal Accident Reporting Systems (FARS), and injuries and PDO crashes estimated by NASS.
5. A recent study conducted for FHWA estimated that the delays caused by urban freeway truck crashes result in nationwide annual costs of $1.6 billion (Bowman and Hummer 1989, 89). The costs were developed from a sample of urban freeways with large total traffic volumes (minimum of 100,000 average daily traffic) and a significant percentage of large-truck traffic (minimum of 5 percent). The results were then expanded to the 1,937 mi of Interstate highway and the 560 mi of freeway that met these criteria.
6. Severe spinal cord injury that is totally disabling is estimated to cost about $1.2 million. The average cost of complete quadriplegia is more than $0.7 million per case (Miller et al. 1989, 309). In comparison, the average monetary cost of a fatality is estimated at $425,400 (Miller et al. 1989, 305).
7. The following costs are assumed using the willingness-to-pay approach: $2,000,000 per fatality, $4,000 per MAIS 1 injury, $31,000 per MAIS 2

injury, \$115,000 per MAIS 3 injury, \$375,000 per MAIS 4 injury, \$1,525,000 per MAIS 5 injury (Miller et al. 1989, 311), and \$1,875 per PDO crash (Miller 1989, A-1). All costs are in 1986 dollars and are applied to 1986 fatalities reported by FARS and injuries and PDO crashes estimated by NASS.

8. Injury rates could not be examined over the same period because NHTSA did not begin collecting data on injuries through NASS until 1979.

9. In 1986 fatality rates were 3.5 per 100 million VMT on rural highways and 1.3 on urban highways (NHTSA 1988a, 3–14). Nearly the reverse pattern was true for injury rates; injury rates were 1.3 injuries per 1 million VMT on rural highways and 2.7 on urban highways (NHTSA 1988b, 16; FHWA 1988b, 171).

10. In 1986 severe injuries (i.e., MAIS $\geq$ 3) represented 7.4 percent of all injuries in rural crashes but only 3.5 percent in urban crashes (NHTSA 1988b, 3–16).

11. NHTSA has reported preliminary figures of 2.2 deaths per 100 million VMT for 1989 (NHTSA 1990b).

12. The projected percent reduction in fatalities is based on an equation developed by Evans (1987) and reprinted in a TRB study (1989, 65), which assumes that the effectiveness of belts in reducing the risk of fatality is 43 percent. The reduction was then applied to an estimated 66,424 fatalities in 2005 based on an average annual travel growth rate of 3 percent.

13. Data for 1983 are used in this comparison because this is the most recent year for which travel estimates by different age groups are available.

14. Large trucks are defined as combination vehicles with three or more axles.

15. In 1988, 40 percent of passenger vehicle occupants were fatally injured in crashes versus 30 percent of light truck occupants.

16. NHTSA now requires head restraints and rear-seat lap and shoulder belts on light trucks and vans. Notices of proposed rulemaking have been issued on side-impact protection, minimum roof crush resistance, and automatic restraint standards (personal communication with Richard Strombotne, NHTSA Office of Vehicle Safety Standards, March 7, 1990).

REFERENCES

ABBREVIATIONS

ACS	American Cancer Society
AHA	American Heart Association
DOT	U.S. Department of Transportation
FHWA	Federal Highway Administration
MVMA	Motor Vehicle Manufacturers Association
NHTSA	National Highway Traffic Safety Administration
NRC	National Research Council
TRB	Transportation Research Board

ACS. 1987. *Cancer Facts and Figures—1987.* New York, N.Y.
AHA. 1987. *1986 Annual Report.* Dallas, Tex.
Accident Facts. 1989. National Safety Council, Chicago, Ill.
Bowman, B.L., and J.E. Hummer. 1989. *Examination of Truck Accidents on*

Urban Freeways. FHWA-RD-89-201. Goodell-Grivas, Inc., Southfield, Mich.; FHWA, U.S. Department of Transportation, Dec., 101 pp.

Census Bureau. 1984. *Projections of the Population by Age, Sex, and Race for the United States, 1983 to 2080.* No. 952, Series P-25. U.S. Department of Commerce.

Census Bureau. 1989. *Statistical Abstract of the United States: 1989,* 109th ed. U.S. Department of Commerce.

Centers for Disease Control. 1990. Years of Potential Life Lost Before Age 65, United States, 1988. *Morbidity and Mortality Weekly Report,* Vol. 39, No. 2, Jan. 19.

Cirillo, J.A. 1968. Interstate System Accident Research: Study II, Interim Report II. *Public Roads,* Vol. 35, No. 3.

Crandall, R.W., H.K. Gruenspecht, T.E. Keeler, and L.B. Lave. 1986. *Regulating the Automobile.* The Brookings Institution, Washington, D.C., 202 pp.

DOT. 1988. *Technical Advisory: Motor Vehicle Accident Costs.* T 75170.1. FHWA, Washington, D.C., June 30.

DOT. 1990. *Moving America: New Directions, New Opportunities.* Feb.

Evans, L. 1987. Estimating Fatality Reductions from Increased Safety Belt Use. *Risk Analysis,* Vol. 7, pp. 49–57.

Evans, L. 1989. *An Attempt to Categorize the Main Determinants of Traffic Safety.* GMR-6645. General Motors Research Laboratories, Warren, Mich., April 5, 26 pp.

Evans, L., M.C. Frick, and R.C. Schwing. 1990. Is it Safer to Fly or Drive? *Risk Analysis,* Vol. 10, No. 2, pp. 239–246.

FHWA. 1985. *Highway Statistics Summary to 1985.* U.S. Department of Transportation.

FHWA. 1988a. *High Priority National Program Area (HPNPA): Work Zone Traffic Control.* Report FHWA-RD-88-216. U.S. Department of Transportation, Aug.

FHWA. 1988b. *Highway Statistics 1987.* U.S. Department of Transportation.

FHWA. 1989. *Highway Statistics 1988.* U.S. Department of Transportation.

Flink, J.J. 1975. *The Car Culture.* The MIT Press, Cambridge, Mass., 260 pp.

Haight, F.A. 1984. Why the Per Capita Traffic Fatality Rate Is Falling. *Journal of Safety Research,* Vol. 15, No. 4, Winter, pp. 137–140.

Hall, J.H., and O.J. Pendleton. 1990. Rural Accident Rate Variations with Traffic Volume. In *Transportation Research Record 1281,* TRB, National Research Council, Washington, D.C.

Hatziandreu, E., J.D. Graham, and M.A. Soto. 1988. AIDS and Biomedical Research Funding: Comparative Analysis. *Reviews of Infectious Diseases,* Vol. 10, No. 1, Jan.–Feb., pp. 159–167.

Hauer, E. 1971. Accidents, Overtaking and Speed Control. *Accident Analysis and Prevention,* Vol. 3, pp. 1–13.

Hauer, E. 1988. Fatal and Injury Accidents—Some Interesting Trends. *The Safety Network,* Vol. 4, No. 3, Dec., pp. 3–5.

Highway Safety Directions. 1990. Young Women and Alcohol. Vol. 2, No. 3, Winter, pp. 4–6.

Jonah, B. (ed.). 1986. Special Issue: Youth and Traffic Accident Risk. *Accident Analysis and Prevention,* Vol. 18, No. 4.

The Liquor Handbook. 1988. Jobson Publishing, New York, N.Y.

Mackay, M. 1988. Crash Protection for Older Persons. In *Special Report 218:*

Transportation in an Aging Society, Vol. 2, TRB, National Research Council, Washington, D.C., pp. 158–193.

Miller, T.R. 1989. *65 mph: Winners and Losers?* The Urban Institute, Washington, D.C.; NHTSA, U.S. Department of Transportation. July.

Miller, T.R., S. Luchter, and C.P. Brinkman. 1989. Crash Costs and Safety Investment. *Accident Prevention and Analysis,* Vol. 21, No. 4, Aug., pp. 305–315.

MVMA. 1977. 1982. 1987. 1989. 1990. *Motor Vehicle Facts and Figures '77, '82, '87, '89, '90.* Detroit, Mich.

National Center for Health Statistics. 1987. Vital Statistics of the United States, Vol. II: Mortality, Part A. In *Accident Facts,* 1989, National Safety Council, Chicago, pp. 8–9.

NHTSA. 1984. *National Accident Sampling System 1982.* Report DOT HS-806-530. U.S. Department of Transportation, March.

NHTSA. 1988a. *Fatal Accident Reporting System 1986.* Report DOT HS-807-245. U.S. Department of Transportation, March.

NHTSA. 1988b. *National Accident Sampling System 1986.* Report DOT HS-807-296. U.S. Department of Transportation, July.

NHTSA. 1989. *Fatal Accident Reporting System 1988.* Report DOT HS-807-507. U.S. Department of Transportation, Dec.

NHTSA. 1990a. *Safety Belt Use Legislative Activity.* Office of Occupant Protection, June 18.

NHTSA. 1990b. *NHTSA Announces Lowest Traffic Fatality Rate in History, Fewer Traffic Deaths in 1989.* U.S. Department of Transportation, Feb. 22.

NRC. 1985. *Injury in America: A Continuing Public Health Problem.* National Academy Press, Washington, D.C., 164 pp.

Partyka, S.C. 1989. Registration-Based Fatality Rates by Car Size from 1978 Through 1987. In *Papers on Car Size—Safety and Trends.* Report DOT HS-807-444. NHTSA, U.S. Department of Transportation, June, pp. 45–72.

Peck, R. 1985. The Role of Youth in Traffic Accidents: A Review of Past and Current California Data. *Alcohol, Drugs, and Driving,* Vol. 1, No. 1–2, Jan–June.

Rice, D.P., E.J. MacKenzie, and Associates. 1989. *Cost of Injury in the United States: A Report to Congress.* Institute for Health and Aging, University of California, San Francisco; Injury Prevention Center, Johns Hopkins University, Baltimore, Md.

Solomon, D. 1964. *Accidents on Main Rural Highways Related to Speed, Driver, and Vehicle.* Bureau of Public Roads, U.S. Department of Commerce, July.

Staplin, L., et al. 1987. *Age-Related Diminished Capabilities and Driver Performance.* Working Paper. FHWA, U.S. Department of Transportation.

TRB. 1988. *Special Report 218: Transportation in an Aging Society,* Vol. 1, National Research Council, Washington, D.C., 125 pp.

TRB. 1989. *Special Report 224: Safety Belts, Airbags, and Child Restraints: Research To Address Emerging Policy Questions.* National Research Council, Washington, D.C., 69 pp.

U.S. Congress. House. 1989. Committee on Public Works and Transportation. *The Status of the Nation's Highways and Bridges: Condition and Performance and Highway Bridge Replacement and Rehabilitation Program 1989.* Committee Print 101-2. Washington, D.C., Government Printing Office, June.

2

Contribution of Research to Highway Safety

T he origins of highway safety research are nearly as old as the motor vehicle itself, but until creation of a federally funded national program of highway safety research in the mid-1960s, research was "fragmentary, inconclusive, and uncoordinated" (U.S. Congress 1956). This overview of highway research activities, with particular emphasis on the research programs of the last two decades, includes the major sponsors of research, the research priorities, illustrations of the role and contribution of research to addressing highway safety problems, funding trends, and current spending on highway safety research. Finally, the adequacy of current programs and funding levels to address the highway safety problems of the next several decades is assessed.

RESPONSIBILITY FOR HIGHWAY SAFETY AND RESEARCH

Highway safety is the responsibility of a broad spectrum of government agencies and private industry (Table 2-1).

Government

The primary roles of government in highway safety are vehicle regulation, highway design and operation, funding and operation of safety programs, and research. Until the mid-1960s highway safety remained the prerogative of individual states, which initiated such programs as driver education, periodic motor vehicle inspection, and driver licensing (TRB 1977, 4). Although the federal government expressed concern about highway safety as early as 1924, when Secretary of Commerce Herbert Hoover held a National Conference on Street and Highway Safety, a strong federal

36

TABLE 2-1   MAJOR SPONSORS OF HIGHWAY SAFETY RESEARCH

Organization	Primary Areas of Emphasis			
	Human	Vehicle	Highway	Other
Federal government				
National Highway Traffic Safety Administration	X	X		X[a]
Federal Highway Administration			X	
Office of Motor Carriers	X	X		X[b]
Centers for Disease Control	X	X		X[c]
States			X[d]	
Private industry				
Automobile manufacturers		X[e]		
Automobile suppliers		X		
Insurance industry	X	X		X[f]
Highway industry			X	

[a] Crash data collection, maintenance, and analysis.
[b] Special regulatory analysis and motor carrier information systems.
[c] Research on trauma and injury mechanisms.
[d] The majority of state sponsored safety research is highway-related but a modest amount of human- and vehicle-related safety research is also conducted.
[e] The majority of the research sponsored by the automobile manufacturers is vehicle-related. However, evaluations of crashes are also undertaken and some research is conducted on driver-related issues, such as alcohol-impaired driving.
[f] Crash analysis.

role did not emerge until the 1960s.[1] A brief rise in motor vehicle fatality rates during the early 1960s, which reversed nearly a decade of progress in reducing the death rate, as well as a political climate of social reform, created an atmosphere ripe for federal intervention.

Legislation enacted by Congress in 1966 defined the federal role in highway safety. The National Traffic and Motor Vehicle Safety Act (P.L. 89-563) authorized the federal government to set national safety standards for motor vehicles. The Highway Safety Act of the same year (P.L. 89-564) provided standards for state programs and funding to address the human- and highway-related aspects of the highway safety problem: Section 402 established national standards to guide state and local highway safety programs and provided grants to support their implementation; Section 403 authorized a program of highway safety research (TRB 1979, 4). The purpose of the latter program was to provide technical support for regulatory activities and general improvement in the knowledge base underlying highway safety activities (TRB 1979, 4). The scope of research and development activities was broadly defined as including, but not limited to, "vehicle, highway, and driver characteristics, accident investigations, communications, emergency medical care, and transportation of the injured" [23 U.S.C. Section 307 (d)].

Organizational responsibilities for federal highway safety programs, including research, were split between two agencies within the U.S. Department of Transportation: the newly created National Highway Traffic Safety Administration (NHTSA) assumed responsibility for vehicle regulation and the human-related aspects of highway safety; the Federal Highway Administration (FHWA) assumed responsibility for safety programs related to highways (TRB 1979, 5) and for regulation of commercial vehicles.[2] The agencies shared responsibility for administering pedestrian safety.

Two new programs have provided additional support for highway safety research since the mid-1980s. The Office of Motor Carriers (OMC) within FHWA received separate funding in 1985 to conduct research in support of its mission to regulate commercial vehicle operators. Also in 1985, a new federally funded research program was created through the Centers for Disease Control (CDC) in Atlanta, Georgia, to address the problem of injury control. The initial pilot program was funded by NHTSA and more than half of the projects were directly related to automotive crash trauma (U.S. Congress 1989, 845). A permanent program was established in 1989, with the majority of the funding from the Department of Health and Human Services. Although the direct funding link with NHTSA was severed, the program continues to conduct research on motor vehicle injuries as the single leading cause of injury death (Rice et al. 1989, 11).

State and local governments also play an important role in highway safety. State governments are the primary administrators of most highway safety programs, such as driver education, periodic motor vehicle inspection, and programs to counter alcohol-impaired driving and encourage safety belt use. In addition, state and local governments program a share of their funds for highway reconstruction, restoration, and rehabilitation, and traffic operations for safety upgrading to improve highway geometrics and remove traffic hazards at potentially dangerous locations. State and local governments also have primary responsibility for enforcing traffic laws and setting appropriate sanctions for noncompliance. Finally, state governments conduct research on highway safety issues. The majority is sponsored by state departments of transportation from earmarked federal Highway Planning and Research (HP&R) funds, which are used primarily to study highway-related safety issues.[3] Departments of motor vehicles and special state safety offices in some states also conduct a modest amount of research on human- and vehicle-related issues.

Private Sector

The automobile manufacturers and suppliers play a primary role in highway safety through the design and engineering of motor vehicles and their component parts. Performance standards for many vehicle safety features are required by federal regulation, but the automobile manufacturers and the larger equipment suppliers also conduct independent research on the safety as well as the performance of their products. The insurance industry contributes directly to highway safety by supporting the Insurance Institute for Highway Safety (IIHS), which conducts research on many aspects of highway safety, often through analyses of crash data. Finally, a modest amount of highly applied research, which could also be considered product development, is conducted by the highway industry, specifically by product suppliers such as manufacturers of guardrails and other barrier devices and of reflective sign and pavement marking materials.

Thus, the responsibility for highway safety and research is widely shared among many organizations with divergent interests, ranging from regulation to product design and development. The research is generally applied,[4] supporting the mission objectives of its sponsoring organizations. The term "research," as it is used in this report, is distinguished from development where possible.[5] In public-sector budgets, research is generally separated from development. In the private sector, however, the distinction is often blurred; research activities are frequently included under the broad category of research and development.

International Organizations

Research has become internationalized, and research in highway safety is no exception. Most of the developed countries have created national research organizations—either public or quasi-public institutions—that conduct research on a broad range of transport topics, including highway safety (Trinca et al. 1988, 52–54). Several foreign automobile manufacturers are noted for their extensive automotive safety research programs. Exchange of research ideas currently takes place though international conferences and journal publications. International cooperation and sharing of research information are necessary to encourage exchange of ideas and broaden the scope of research currently being conducted in the United States.

RESEARCH PRIORITIES

In the last 20 years, research has been conducted on each of the principal elements affecting highway safety—the human, the vehicle, and the highway—and supporting data bases have been developed. The major research programs in each of these areas are summarized in this section.

(A more detailed history of highway safety research programs can be found in Appendix A.)

Driver and Pedestrian Safety

Driver error or inappropriate driving behavior is a major contributing factor to motor vehicle crashes. Three in-depth studies of crashes dating from the 1970s (Perchonok 1972; Sabey 1973; Treat et al. 1979) identified human error or deficiency as a major factor in roughly 60 to 90 percent of the crashes, environmental factors (weather, road condition, signing, lighting, etc.) in roughly 12 to 35 percent of the crashes, and vehicle equipment failures in about 5 to 20 percent of the crashes.

During the past two decades, NHTSA has been the chief sponsor of research on the role of the driver and cosponsor with FHWA on the role of the pedestrian in motor vehicle crashes. Program activities peaked during the mid-1970s when research budgets reached nearly $5 million (Table A-1), supporting multiyear programs in alcohol and pedestrian research.

Alcohol-impaired driving was identified as a problem of major proportions early in the agency's history in a report to Congress in 1968 by the Secretary of Transportation (U.S. Congress 1968). Research was conducted on the effects of alcohol on driver performance, on alternative enforcement and sanctioning strategies for deterring the general population from driving while impaired, and on improved methods for reliable police detection of alcohol-impaired drivers.

Another important initiative during the 1970s was the pedestrian research program. Crashes involving pedestrians were first analyzed to provide a typology of major crash types, and countermeasures were developed for each of these types. Limited field testing was conducted of the countermeasures, the most promising of which formed the basis for extensive multiyear demonstration projects.

NHTSA's early program activities also involved research related to driver-oriented programs administered by state and local governments, such as driver education and training and driver licensing. The thrust of the research was on achieving results that would have practical application in state and community program operations. NHTSA's remaining research funds during the 1970s were allocated among occupant restraint programs (examining public acceptability of automatic safety restraints and mandatory safety belt use laws), speeding and other unsafe driving actions, and motorcycle safety (including testing and licensing, education, and helmet use).

In 1981 NHTSA's driver and pedestrian research program was cut by more than one-half from its level during the 1970s and concentrated in two areas—occupant protection and alcohol abuse. Together, these areas have received two-thirds of the funds available for behavioral research since the inception of the NHTSA research program (Table A-1).

In FY1988 and 1989, budgetary increases of $200,000 and $1 million, respectively, permitted a broadening of the research agenda to include research on older drivers and on speed monitoring and enforcement to track the impact of raising the speed limit on rural Interstates. However, funding has been sporadic. For example, funding for research on older drivers in NHTSA's FY 1990 budget dropped by nearly 50 percent from 1989 levels to $160,000 (personal communication with Director, Office of Driver and Pedestrian Research, October 9, 1990).

Funding of behavioral research outside of NHTSA is limited. The CDC injury control program has provided some new resources for behavioral research under the category of injury prevention, such as increasing bicycle helmet and safety belt use among children. A few states conduct research on driver-related issues. For example, the California Department of Motor Vehicles has a long history of research on the relationship between driver characteristics and crash involvement. Behavioral issues have not been a significant component of private research budgets (U.S. Congress 1989, 1036).

Vehicle-Related Safety

The primary impetus for research on motor vehicle safety was the National Traffic and Motor Vehicle Safety Act of 1966, which empowered NHTSA to set minimum vehicle safety performance standards. With a mandate to act, NHTSA moved quickly to develop the first regulations. Within 2 years of its creation, NHTSA had issued 29 motor vehicle safety standards and had proposed 95 more (Graham 1989, 32).

Following this first round of standard-setting, NHTSA began to develop a research program in motor vehicle safety to support its regulatory mission. Top priority was given to research on measures to improve vehicle crashworthiness. Because of the large number of fatalities and injuries in frontal crashes, early crashworthiness research focused on methods for reducing injury in frontal collisions through demonstration of airbag technologies and development of anthropometric test devices (i.e., crash dummies).

During the mid-1970s research emphasis shifted to mitigating injuries in side-impact crashes and, more recently, in rollover crashes. Today crashworthiness research on side impacts, rollovers, and improved frontal protection represents nearly 50 percent of NHTSA's vehicle research budget (estimates provided by NHTSA).

Research in biomechanics—that is, the study of injury mechanisms and human tolerances to trauma—provides the basic knowledge to support the development of testing devices and, from these, performance standards for testing vehicle crashworthiness. Early NHTSA-sponsored research, which drew on previous biomechanical research sponsored mainly by General Motors (GM), developed criteria to test injury tolerance and establish standards for occupant protection in frontal crashes. More recently NHTSA has applied acceleration-based criteria to measure the risk of injury in side-impacts, developed a side-impact dummy, and proposed an amended side-impact performance standard (*Federal Register* 1988). GM is critical of the criteria and dummy as predictors of injury risk in a side impact (GMRL 1989, 4–5; Viano et al. 1989b).

The biomechanics research field is small with few trained scientists and engineers with background and experience in the mechanics and physiology of trauma (Viano et al. 1989a, 413). Moreover, current agency funding of about $2 million annually for biomechanics (representing about 15 percent of NHTSA's vehicle research budget) and about $1.7 million more annually from the CDC injury control program is spread widely in small contracts that do not provide for the long-term testing and research needed to make further major advances in vehicle crashworthiness in a timely manner.

Crash avoidance, which includes research to support vehicle regulation, is currently funded at slightly more than one-third of NHTSA's current vehicle research budget. Crash avoidance has traditionally taken a secondary role in the research program, in part because of the complexity of factors contributing to crashes and the difficulty of identifying for study those interventions with the greatest potential for reducing crash risk (Finkelstein 1989, 2–3). For example, although driver error is often cited as the primary cause of crashes, a wide range of interventions, such as better driver training or improvements to make the vehicle or the highway more forgiving, could all reduce the likelihood of a crash.

NHTSA's crash avoidance research program has focused on technology improvements (e.g., improved lighting, particularly brake lighting, and improved tire and brake performance), but even here research is lagging technology development. "Head-up" display driver information systems, which provide the driver with essential information within his field of vision, radar warning systems, and the like are in development or are already being offered in special vehicle models. An adequate assessment of their safety implications requires a more extensive program of human factors research (i.e., research that bridges psychology and engineering) than the current $1 million budgeted by NHTSA and FHWA (estimate provided by the agencies).

Private industry, particularly the automobile manufacturers, has also devoted considerable resources to vehicle crashworthiness research over the last two decades through testing, developing computer simulation models, and conducting biomechanics research (GMRL 1988). Although information on the level of private spending for research is proprietary, GM's program is generally thought to be the largest both in terms of its research staff and the level of its researchers' contributions to the technical literature (GMRL 1988, 1).

Highway-Related Safety

FHWA has sole responsibility for three highway-related safety areas—identification and surveillance of crash locations; highway design, construction, and maintenance; and traffic engineering—and shares responsibility for a fourth, pedestrian safety, with NHTSA.

During the 1970s, FHWA's yearly highway safety research budget of approximately $9 million supported several multiyear programs of research. From the start, FHWA emphasized research on practical problems that could readily be incorporated into engineering practice. A $10 million, 10-year research program was begun in 1970 on wet weather crashes and skid resistance after crash analyses had identified wet weather conditions as a major environmental factor contributing to crashes. A research program was also initiated on roadside safety, an outgrowth of research during the mid-1960s on improved designs for signs on Interstate highways. Since 1970, FHWA has spent nearly $15 million for research on roadside safety devices, such as breakaway sign and luminaire supports, recovery zones, and protective guardrails and barriers, to protect motorists (TRB staff estimate based on Annual Progress Reports of the Federally Coordinated Program of Highway Research, Development, and Technology).

As the emphasis of the federal highway program moved from new construction to reconstruction, so did FHWA's highway safety research agenda. Several research studies were initiated in 1978 on work-zone safety in anticipation of growing hazards from rehabilitation activities in high-traffic areas. The rapid increase in truck travel during the mid-1970s provided the impetus for another new program of research, on large-truck safety.

FHWA's safety research budget was reduced by one-third during the 1980s and research programs were concentrated on high-priority, short-term problems (i.e., those that could be solved in 3 to 5 years), such as reflectivity of traffic control signs and pavement markings.

FHWA is planning a far more ambitious research agenda for the 1990s if new funding for research is made available in the reauthorizing legislation for the highway program in 1991 (FHWA 1989b). More emphasis would be given to a broad program of human factors research to identify and understand incompatibilities between driver capabilities and limitations (fatigue, older drivers) and highway design (intersections, freeway interchanges). As part of FHWA's emerging interest in developing intelligent vehicle-highway system (IVHS) technology to alleviate congestion, the agency would also examine the effects of this new technology on safety. Because of NHTSA's related interest in human factors research and new vehicle technologies, an effective program would require more coordination between the two agencies' research programs than there has been in the past.

States have also spent large sums, primarily from their HP&R funds, on highway-related safety research studies. However, with the exception of pooled-fund projects through the National Cooperative Highway Research Program, the funds are widely spread among individual states and often focus on very localized problems. For example, nearly one-fourth of the safety-related HP&R projects in FY1988 were evaluations of the performance of specific roadside safety hardware, including crash testing of bridge rails and breakaway barricades.

Private companies have also conducted research in conjunction with development of highway safety-related products, such as barrier systems, reflective pavement marking materials, and deicing chemicals.

Data-Related Activities

NHTSA has developed the primary data bases that are critical to support research and management of highway safety programs. The oldest is the Fatal Accident Reporting System (FARS). In operation since 1975, FARS provides a census of fatal traffic crashes that occur each year; fatal crashes are defined as those that involve at least one fatality within 30 days of a crash (NHTSA 1989, Foreword).

A companion data base to provide information on nonfatal crashes, the National Accident Sampling System (NASS), has been in operation since 1979. NASS was recently restructured into two data collection systems in an effort to reduce costs and tailor the system to meet user needs: (a) a General Estimates System to provide national estimates of crashes by type from police accident reports without intensive follow-up crash investigations and (b) a Crashworthiness Data System based on detailed information of a small sample of crashes to support research directly related to injury and crashworthiness of passenger vehicles, light trucks, and vans. Other specialized data files, such as the Crash Avoidance Research Data File (CARDfile), have been developed to support research in other areas, such as crash avoidance.

The National Center for Statistics and Analysis of NHTSA, which administers the data bases, conducts in-house analyses of crash data to define the magnitude of specific safety problems, provide supporting information on regulatory initiatives, and evaluate specific safety counter-measures. From time to time, it may also conduct in-depth crash investi-gations on topics of priority interest, such as high-severity crashes of cars equipped with airbags and other automatic restraint systems.

In part because of the change in the scope of NASS to focus on pas-senger vehicle crashworthiness, FHWA is developing a Highway Safety Information System to provide more data on highway characteristics that will assist in defining appropriate countermeasures. Building on data already collected by the states, a prototype system is being developed using crash, traffic, and roadway data from five states (FHWA 1989a, 2).

ILLUSTRATIVE ACCOMPLISHMENTS

The last several decades of research have yielded enormous improvements in highway safety. New vehicles, although smaller than their counterparts of the late 1960s and early 1970s, now include a wide array of crash-worthiness features that research has demonstrated as highly effective in reducing traffic injury and death. The highway itself has become less hazardous as researchers have developed more forgiving barrier systems and roadside hardware that breaks away on impact. Perhaps the most important highway-related improvement is the Interstate highway system, which embodied state-of-the-art design improvements at the time of its construction. Improvements in emergency medical services and response times and development of regionalized trauma care centers have reduced the number of traffic deaths that researchers had identified as preventable with timely medical assistance (Boyd 1983; West et al. 1983; Cales 1984; Cales and Trunkey 1985; Shackford et al. 1986). Reductions in alcohol-related motor vehicle fatalities are attributed in part to countermeasures developed from research on appropriate interventions to deter alcohol-impaired driving (Fell and Nash 1989). The list could go on.

The role and payoffs of research are described for one of these areas—developing motor vehicle crashworthiness and crash avoidance standards. The crashworthiness standards, adopted by NHTSA beginning in 1967, have as a group reduced deaths and injuries from motor vehicle crashes and have been found to be cost-beneficial (Crandall et al. 1986; Graham and Garber 1984; Robertson 1981).[6] Research has played a direct role in the development of many of these standards, either by suggesting innova-tions or by refining concepts in the laboratory that led to safer designs and ultimately to cost-beneficial safety standards.

Biomechanics and Vehicle Crashworthiness

In the late 1950s, GM began developing an energy-absorbing steering column that would compress in a frontal crash to absorb most of the energy of the collision between the driver and the steering system. The key question from designers was how much resistance the column should offer to cushion the impact and reduce injury risk for the largest number of drivers. A column that offered too little resistance would not provide any significant cushion in a high-speed collision; one that offered too much resistance would not help in a low-speed collision. Because information to answer the question was not available, GM Research Laboratories and Wayne State University developed a collaborative program to develop measures of human tolerance to injury (Viano 1987). Sled tests with embalmed cadavers provided basic information about head, chest, and knee skeletal tolerance. Tests of rib cage fractures by Gadd and Patrick (1968) led to tolerance estimates that allowed the energy-absorbing steering column to be developed. Energy-absorbing steering columns were required by NHTSA beginning in 1968. A later evaluation found them to be responsible for a 38 percent reduction in injuries caused by contact with the steering wheel (Kahane 1984). Before the increase in safety belt use brought about by passage of state mandatory safety belt use laws, the energy-absorbing steering column was reported to be the single most effective safety standard, reducing the risk of fatality in frontal crashes by 12 percent (Kahane 1984; Viano 1987).

Biomechanics research also played a major part in the development of the high-penetration-resistant windshield (Viano 1987). Research in the 1960s had shown that windshields then in use were the source of many serious facial injuries. The automobile manufacturers and their suppliers supported a research program at Wayne State University to develop a windshield that would yield more on impact and resist penetration of the head. Researchers at Wayne State conducted head impact experiments and developed a rough measure of the tolerance of the skull to concussion. Designers used the information on tolerance to develop a windshield with an inner layer of plastic that would provide sufficient yield during impact to cushion the head and reduce injury. High-penetration-resistant windshield glazing (required by NHTSA effective 1968) and better bonding of the windshield to the body (required by NHTSA effective 1970) were found by NHTSA to have reduced serious facial lacerations and fractures by 70 percent (Kahane 1985).

Biomechanics research has had other benefits as well. The early research on head impacts by GM led to the precursor to the present Head Impact Criterion (HIC), which is used to measure new-vehicle compliance with NHTSA's frontal crash occupant protection requirements. Offshoots of this research have also been used in the testing and development of several other safety innovations, including airbags (Viano 1987).

Human Factors and the Center High-Mounted Stoplight

NHTSA's requirement that all cars sold after September 1985 be equipped with center high-mounted stoplights is proving to be a very cost-effective standard (Kahane 1987, 1989). Relatively few fatalities result from rear impacts (about 5 percent), but about 20 percent of nonfatal injuries in police-reported crashes involve rear impacts (Kahane 1989). Although the new stoplight will cost consumers $100 million a year, Kahane estimates that it will save $910 million annually in property damage by reducing rear-end collisions by 17 percent (Kahane 1989, ix). This cost-beneficial device resulted from about 20 years of research on improving the performance of rear lighting systems. The total cost of the NHTSA-funded research was less than $5 million.

In the late 1960s the U.S. Department of Transportation began funding developmental research to improve rear-lighting signaling systems (Digges et al. 1985). The early human factors studies tested alternative designs with early driving simulators and on-road tests. This research, coupled with complementary, but independent, university and industry research, pointed to the need for a single brake light mounted higher than existing lamps. The prevailing rear lights at the time used a single lamp that varied in intensity to convey the message of turning, braking, or running. Researchers advocated instead a single lamp dedicated to braking that would be closer to the center of the following driver's field of view.

Once a consensus had been reached on the need for a dedicated high-mounted stoplight, field tests were initiated by both NHTSA and IIHS. The NHTSA-sponsored test of a Washington, D.C., cab fleet equipped with center high-mounted stoplights showed a more than 50 percent reduction in rear-end collisions (Malone et al. 1978). A follow-up study sponsored by IIHS equipped 600 New York City cabs with the stoplights and used 300 cabs as a control group (Rausch et al. 1982). The results were quite consistent with those of the earlier NHTSA study—a 44 to 58 percent reduction in rear-end collisions.

Since the standard was issued in 1985, NHTSA has performed two evaluations. A preliminary appraisal found that the likelihood of being struck from the rear while braking was 22 percent lower for 1986 model year cars equipped with the stoplights than for 1985 model year cars not so equipped (Kahane 1987). A follow-up evaluation in which 1980–1985 model year cars were compared with 1986–1987 model year cars found a 17 percent reduction in rear-end collisions (Kahane 1989). On the basis of this level of effectiveness, up to 80,000 injuries and $910 million in property damage will be avoided each year once all cars have center high-mounted stoplights (Kahane 1989, ix). A recent study (McKnight et al. 1989) has also found a beneficial effect, measured by a reduction in brake response time for vans, pickups, and light trucks equipped with center high-mounted stoplights. Although this study did not estimate the benefits from reductions in rear-end collisions, NHTSA has begun rulemaking to require center high-mounted stoplights on these vehicles.

FUNDING TRENDS

Research has contributed important improvements in highway safety, as the previous section has illustrated. However, a review of funding levels and spending by major categories of research over the past 15 to 20 years indicates a declining level of effort, which raises questions about the adequacy of current research programs to continue this progress.

Historical Funding

Historical figures are available for one major source of funds for highway safety research, the federal government. Figure 2-1 traces total federal funding for highway safety research in current and constant dollars for the past 15 years.[7] Funding sources include Section 403 of the Highway Safety Act of 1966, which is administered by NHTSA and FHWA; appropriations for the research program of OMC (since FY1985); and appropriations for the injury control program administered by CDC (since FY1986).[8]

The total level of federal funds available for highway safety research has declined significantly over this period despite the infusion of new resources since the mid-1980s. Funding averaged about $55 million annually in inflation-adjusted dollars between 1975 and 1981, but declined to an annual average of about $35 million after 1981—a reduction of nearly 40 percent.

An analysis of funding by major research category, which is possible for the two largest sources of federal funding (i.e., NHTSA[9] and FHWA appropriations), provides a good indication of research priorities and how these have changed over the past two decades (Figure 2-2). The dominance of vehicle-related research during the 1970s is evident. Although average annual funding for this purpose has dropped by more than half in real terms since 1981, vehicle-related research continues to be the largest funding category with the exception of funding for NHTSA's data bases.

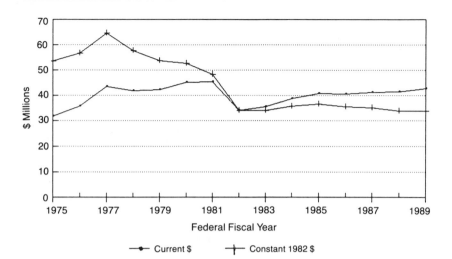

FIGURE 2-1   Total federal spending for highway safety research, 1975–1989; figures are deflated using the GNP price deflator as reported in the U.S. Budget (data from Associate Administrator for Research and Development, NHTSA; Office of Fiscal Services and Office of Motor Carriers, FHWA; and Assistant Director for Extramural Research, CDC).

Highway-related safety research is another important funding category, but since 1981, average annual funding has been nearly half that of earlier levels (Figure 2-2). In comparison, driver- and pedestrian-related research has never been a large program area, even in the 1970s when average annual funding levels were more than twice those of the 1980s. Data development and maintenance, which is an appropriate federal activity, is the only area that has grown in real terms over the last two decades to become the single largest funding category during the 1980s. These funds were expended primarily on NHTSA's data bases, FARS and NASS, which support not only research but also the management and monitoring of highway safety programs. Including them as part of total funding for highway safety research overstates the amount of funds that is actually being used to support research.

Current Spending

Funding for highway safety research from public budgets reached nearly $70 million in 1989 (Table 2-2). Table 2-2 does not include safety research funded by the private sector; the automobile manufacturers, automobile suppliers and suppliers of highway appurtenances, and the insur-

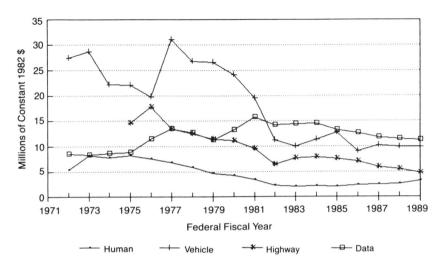

FIGURE 2-2   Appropriations for NHTSA and FHWA by major category of highway safety research, 1975–1989; figures are deflated using the GNP price deflator as reported in the U.S. Budget (data from Associate Administrator for Research, NHTSA; and Office of Fiscal Services, FHWA).

ance industry typically do not report their spending on this activity. Nor does it include the budgets of agencies that fund research on issues related to highway safety, such as alcohol abuse or vision.[10]

The federal government is a major sponsor of research, accounting for more than three-fourths of all reported funding in 1989 (Table 2-2). NHTSA has the single largest safety research budget from its share of Section 403 funds.

Individual states are the other major sponsor of highway safety research, with estimated funding of more than $16 million, or nearly 25 percent of total reported funding in 1989 (Table 2-2). However, the funds are spread widely among the states. The majority of projects are selected at state discretion using HP&R funds, and many focus on state-specific highway safety issues.

Spending on highway safety research is disproportionate to the size of the problem. Current annual highway safety research budgets of $70 million represent about one-tenth of 1 percent of the annual medical expenditures, lost wages, and property damage cost associated with traffic crashes. The nation is investing less than 30 cents per capita each year in research to identify ways of reducing this societal burden.

Moreover, this level of public investment in research falls far short of comparable public investment[11] in research on other major public health problems. For example, research spending per potential year of work life

TABLE 2-2   SUMMARY OF FUNDING FOR HIGHWAY SAFETY
RESEARCH, 1989

Organization	Funding ($ millions)
Federal	
National Highway Traffic Safety Administration	40.8[a]
Federal Highway Administration	6.1[b]
Office of Motor Carriers	1.9[c]
Centers for Disease Control	3.9[d]
Subtotal	52.7
State agencies	
Federally funded HP&R	10.3[e]
State-matched HP&R	1.3[f]
100 percent state funded	4.9[g]
Subtotal	16.5
Private industry	
Insurance industry	—[h]
Automotive industry	—[h]
Highway industry	—[h]
Grand total	69.2

[a] NHTSA share of Section 403 appropriations. Figures include R&D budget as compiled by Associate Administrator for Research and Development, NHTSA (May 10, 1989), plus salaries and expenses for related NHTSA personnel as shown in NHTSA Budget Estimates for Fiscal Year 1990 (p. 98).
[b] FHWA share of Section 403 appropriations as reported by Office of Fiscal Services, Budget Division.
[c] Appropriations for research.
[d] Share of funding for Injury Prevention Research Centers and individual research grants that is motor vehicle related (estimates provided by Assistant Director for Extramural Research, CDC, April 4, 1990).
[e] Includes National Cooperative Highway Research Program projects, other pooled fund projects, and individual state HP&R research projects, which totaled $68 million in FY1988, the latest year for which data are available. According to FHWA, approximately 15 percent of these funds was spent on safety research.
[f] State match for HP&R funds is 15 percent ($8.7 million), of which about 15 percent is spent on safety-related research.
[g] Based on figures provided by FHWA and a sample of state highway and motor vehicle departments.
[h] Not available; proprietary information.

lost is roughly 8 times as much on heart disease and nearly 17 times as much on cancer (see Figure ES-1). And focusing on fatalities ignores the injuries, particularly the permanently disabling brain and spinal cord injuries, and extensive property damage that also result from motor vehicle crashes.

SUMMARY

Creation of a federally funded national program of highway safety research in the mid-1960s as part of the legislative package accompanying federal regulation of motor vehicle safety and state highway safety programs brought a new focus to research in the decades that followed. Research was conducted on each of the principal elements affecting highway safety—the human, the vehicle, and the highway—and the research has paid off. It played a direct role, for example, in the development and evaluation of vehicle crashworthiness standards, which, as a group, have been considered a highly cost-beneficial investment.

The federal government is a major sponsor of highway safety research. However, since 1981, average annual federal funding for highway safety research has dropped by nearly 40 percent in inflation-adjusted dollars from the average annual federal funding levels of the period between 1975 and 1981. The total current level of spending on highway safety research, which includes state-sponsored but not privately funded research, is approximately $70 million. This level of effort is disproportionate to the size of the highway safety problem and public investment in research on other major public health problems.

Reduced levels of federal support during the 1980s have diminished capacity to sustain research and researchers in certain areas that are critical to advancing the knowledge base so that the safety community can effectively address the emerging safety problems of the next several decades. For example, the current deployment of funding for biomechanics research is inadequate to support the long-term testing and research needed to make major new breakthroughs in vehicle crashworthiness. Similarly, funding for human factors research is not sufficient to assess fully the safety of new driver information and vehicle control technologies that have the potential to reduce collision risk. More innovative approaches are also needed if persistent problems in highway safety are to be confronted aggressively. Research to address emerging highway safety problems is addressed in Chapter 3. In Chapter 4, areas for continuing research on persistent highway safety problems are examined.

NOTES

1. The U.S. Public Health Service did provide funding for highway safety research before the 1960s, but funding levels were modest.
2. For a short period (1967 to 1970) responsibilities for all highway safety activities were merged under a single entity, the National Highway Safety Bureau within FHWA. However, when the Federal-Aid Highway Act of 1970 elevated the bureau to a separate administration independent of FHWA, renamed the National Highway Traffic Safety Administration, responsibilities were once again split (TRB 1979, 4–5).
3. The Hayden-Cartwright Act of 1934 laid the foundation for state-sponsored highway planning and research activities by authorizing a $1\frac{1}{2}$ percent set-aside of federal apportionments for this purpose (FHWA 1976, 321).

Research was specifically identified as an eligible activity in the Federal-Aid Highway Act of 1944; the Federal-Aid Highway Act of 1962 restricted the set-aside for research and planning purposes only (FHWA 1976, 321).

4. The National Science Foundation defines applied research as research directed toward gaining "knowledge or understanding necessary for determining the means by which a recognized and specific need may be met" (National Science Foundation 1988, 34). In contrast, basic research is defined as "research directed toward increases in knowledge or understanding of the subject under study without specific application towards processes or products in mind" (National Science Foundation 1988, 34).

5. The National Science Foundation defines development, as distinguished from research, as "the systematic use of the knowledge or understanding gained from research directed toward the production of useful materials, devices, systems or methods, including design and development of prototypes and processes" (National Science Foundation 1988, 34).

6. One author of *Regulation of the Automobile* (Crandall et al. 1986), Lester Lave, notes, however, that there are large differences in the net benefits of individual safety features. He cautions that although it is difficult to estimate the benefits and costs of individual safety standards, it is important not to impose standards that have a negative net benefit.

7. Between 1974 and 1981, $35.6 million in research and evaluation related to Emergency Medical Services (EMS) programs was funded by the EMS research program established under Title XII of the Public Health Services Act and administered by the National Center for Health Services Research (Agency for Health Care Policy and Research, staff compilation from published program reports). Annual estimates of the share of research that was motor vehicle related could not be isolated, and thus these funds were not reported in Figure 2-1.

8. Between FY1986 and FY1989, OMC and CDC appropriations represented between 7.5 and 9.5 percent of total federal appropriations for highway safety. OMC appropriations in current dollars were $1.2 million in FY1985, $0.9 million in FY1986, $1.6 million in FY1987, $1.9 million in FY1988, and $1.9 million in FY1989. CDC appropriations for motor vehicle-related injury research (grant funds and center funds) in current dollars were $4.2 million in FY1986, $3.9 million in FY1987, $3.7 million in FY1988, and $3.9 million in FY1989. The designation of CDC projects as motor vehicle related was determined by the Assistant Director for Extramural Research, CDC, April 4, 1990.

9. Appropriations for NHTSA are for contract research and do not include staff and administrative costs.

10. For example, several agencies fund research on injuries, such as the National Institute for Occupational Safety and Health, the National Institute of General Medical Services and the National Institute of Neurological and Communicative Disorders and Stroke of the National Institutes of Health, the National Institute on Alcohol Abuse and Alcoholism, and the National Institute for Disability and Rehabilitative Research of the U.S. Department of Education. Some of the research may be applicable to motor vehicle injuries (personal communication with the Director, Division of Injury Epidemiology and Control, Centers for Disease Control, July 17, 1989).

11. Only public funding for research was included here, because funding by the private sector on highway safety research is not reported. Private funding for

research on cancer by the American Cancer Society was $89 million in 1988. Private funding for research on heart disease by the American Heart Association was $65 million in the same year. FY1988 was selected for the comparisons because that was the latest year for which data on potential years of work life lost were available.

REFERENCES

ABBREVIATIONS

FHWA	Federal Highway Administration
GMRL	General Motors Research Laboratories
NHTSA	National Highway Traffic Safety Administration
TRB	Transportation Research Board

Boyd, D.R. 1983. The History of Emergency Medical Services Systems (EMS) in the United States of America. In *Systems Approach to Emergency Care* (D.R. Boyd, R.F. Edlich, and S.H. Micik, eds.), Appleton-Century-Crofts, Norwalk, Conn., pp. 1–82.

Cales, R.H. 1984. Trauma Mortality in Orange County: The Effect of Implementation of a Regional Trauma System. *Annals of Emergency Medicine,* Vol. 13, pp. 1–10.

Cales, R.H., and D.D. Trunkey. 1985. Preventable Trauma Deaths: A Review of Trauma Care Systems Development. *Journal of the American Medical Association,* Vol. 254, No. 8, pp. 1059–1063.

Crandall, R., H. Gruenspecht, T. Keeler, and L. Lave. 1986. *Regulation of the Automobile.* The Brookings Institution, Washington, D.C.

Digges, K.H., R. Nicholson, and E. Rouse. 1985. *The Technical Basis for the Center High Mounted Stoplamp.* SAE 851240. Society of Automotive Engineers, Warrendale, Pa.

Federal Register. 1988. Vol. 53, No. 17, Jan. 27, pp. 2,239–2,260.

Fell, J.C., and C.E. Nash. 1989. The Nature of the Alcohol Problem in U.S. Fatal Crashes. *Health Education Quarterly,* Vol. 16, No. 3, Fall, pp. 335–343.

FHWA. 1976. *America's Highways: 1776–1976.* U.S. Department of Transportation.

FHWA. 1989a. *High Priority National Program Area (HPNPA): Information Resources.* Report FHWA-RD-88-221. U.S. Department of Transportation, Jan.

FHWA. 1989b. *A Program for Post-91 Highway Safety and Traffic Operations.* Internal draft. U.S. Department of Transportation, July.

Finkelstein, M. 1989. *Future Motor Vehicle Safety Research Needs: Crash Avoidance.* Presented at the 12th International Technical Conference on Experimental Safety Vehicles, Gothenburg, Sweden, May 29–June 1.

Gadd, C.W., and L.M. Patrick. 1968. *Systems versus Laboratory Impact Tests for Estimating Injury Hazard.* SAE 6800053. Society of Automotive Engineers, Warrendale, Pa.

GMRL. 1988. Safety Research at the General Motors Research Laboratories: Examining the Causes and Control of Automotive Crashes and Injury. *Search,* Vol. 23, No. 3, July–August.

GMRL. 1989. Side-Impact Protection: GM Tackles the "Next Safety Frontier." *Search*, Vol. 24, No. 3, July–August.

Graham, J.D. 1989. *Auto Safety: Assessing America's Performance*. Auburn House Publishing Co., Dover, Mass.

Graham, J.D., and S. Garber. 1984. Evaluating the Effects of Automobile Safety Regulations. *Journal of Policy Analysis and Management*, Vol. 3, Winter, pp. 206–224.

Kahane, C.J. 1984. *The National Highway Traffic Safety Administration's Evaluations of Motor Vehicle Safety Standards*. SAE 84092. Society of Automotive Engineers, Warrendale, Pa.

Kahane, C.J. 1985. *An Evaluation of Windshield Glazing and Installation Methods for Passenger Cars*. Report DOT-HS-806-639. NHTSA, U.S. Department of Transportation.

Kahane, C.J. 1987. *The Effectiveness of Center High Mounted Stop Lights: A Preliminary Evaluation*. Report DOT-HS-806-890. NHTSA, U.S. Department of Transportation.

Kahane, C.J. 1989. *An Evaluation of Center High Mounted Stop Lamps Based on 1987 Data*. Report DOT-HS-807-442. NHTSA, U.S. Department of Transportation.

Malone, T., M. Kirkpatrick, J. Kohl, and C. Baker. 1978. *Field Test Evaluation of Rear Lighting Systems*. Report NHTSA-HS-5-01228. NHTSA, U.S. Department of Transportation.

McKnight, A.J., D. Shinar, and A. Reizes. 1989. *The Effects of the Center High-Mounted Stop Lamp on Vans and Trucks*. Report DOT-HS-807-506. NHTSA, U.S. Department of Transportation, May, 33 pp.

National Science Foundation. 1988. *National Patterns of Science and Technology Resources: 1987*. Report NSF 88-305. Washington, D.C.

NHTSA. 1989. *Fatal Accident Reporting System 1988*. Report DOT-HS-807-507. U.S. Department of Transportation, Dec.

NHTSA. 1990. *Budget Estimates for Fiscal Year 1990 Submitted to Committee on Appropriations*. U.S. Department of Transportation.

Perchonok, K. 1972. *Accident Cause Analysis*. Cornell Aeronautical Laboratory, Inc., Ithaca, New York, July.

Rausch, A., J. Wong, and M. Kirkpatrick. 1982. A Field Test of Two Single Center High Mounted Brake Light Systems. *Accident Analysis and Prevention*, Vol. 14, No. 4, pp. 287–291.

Rice, D.P., E.J. MacKenzie, and Associates. 1989. *Cost of Injury in the United States: A Report to Congress*. Institute for Health and Aging, University of California, San Francisco; Injury Prevention Center, Johns Hopkins University, Baltimore, Md.

Robertson, L.S. 1981. Automobile Safety Regulations and Death Reductions in the United States. *American Journal of Public Health*, Vol. 71, pp. 818–822.

Sabey, B. 1973. *Accident Analysis in Great Britain*. U.K. Transport and Road Research Laboratory, Crowthorne, Berkshire, Oct.

Shackford, S.R., P. Hollingworth-Fridlund, G.F. Cooper, and A.B. Eastman. 1986. The Effect of Regionalization upon the Quality of Trauma Care as Assessed by Concurrent Audit Before and After Institution of a Trauma System: A Preliminary Report. *Journal of Trauma*, Vol. 26, No. 9, Sept., pp. 812–820.

TRB. 1977. *Special Report 178: The Future of the National Highway Safety Program*. National Research Council, Washington, D.C., 43 pp.

TRB. 1979. *Highway Safety Research, Development, and Demonstration: Conference Proceedings.* Unpublished Report 16. National Research Council, Washington, D.C., Dec., 129 pp.

Treat, J.R., et al. 1979. *Tri-Level Study of the Causes of Traffic Accidents.* 1979. Report DOT HS-034-3-545. Indiana University, Bloomington.

Trinca, G., I. Johnston, B. Campbell, F. Haight, P. Knight, M. Mackay, J. McLean, and E. Petrucelli. 1988. *Reducing Traffic Injury: A Global Challenge.* Royal Australian College of Surgeons, A.H., Massina & Co., Melbourne, Australia, 136 pp.

U.S. Congress. House. 1956. Testimony of the National Safety Council at Traffic Safety Hearings before Committee on Interstate and Foreign Commerce. Cited in Eastman, J.W., 1984, *Styling vs. Safety,* University Press of America, Inc., Lanham, Md., p. 158.

U.S. Congress. House. Committee on Public Works. 1968. *1968 Alcohol and Highway Safety Report.* Committee Print 90-34. 90th Congress, Second Session.

U.S. Congress. House. Committee on Appropriations. 1989. Department of Transportation and Related Agencies Appropriations for 1990. Hearings . . . 101st Congress, First Session, Part 4.

Viano, D. C. 1987. *Cause and Control of Automotive Trauma.* General Motors Research Laboratories. GMR 5900. Warren, Mich.

Viano, D.C., A.I. King, J.W. Melvin, and K. Weber. 1989a. Injury Biomechanics Research: An Essential Element in the Prevention of Trauma. *Journal of Biomechanics,* Vol. 22, No. 5, pp. 403–417.

Viano, D.C., I.V. Lau, D.V. Andrzejak, and C. Asbury. 1989b. Biomechanics of Injury in Lateral Impacts. *Accident Prevention and Analysis,* Vol. 21, No. 6, Dec. pp. 535–551.

West, J.G., R.H. Cales, and A.B. Gazzaniga. 1983. Impact of Regionalization: The Orange County Experience. *Archives of Surgery,* Vol. 118, pp. 740–744.

3

Research To Address Emerging Highway Safety Problems

Meeting the highway safety problems that are likely to emerge over the next several decades requires innovative solutions that can be developed by research. A prerequisite for effective research is a well-structured research program in highway safety; current research programs fall short in key areas, as will be shown. If emerging problems are to be anticipated before they become serious, research should begin now on a series of topics that could enhance current understanding of safety in a changing travel environment.

A WELL-STRUCTURED RESEARCH PROGRAM

Advancing knowledge through research requires sustained support and a breadth of scope that can range from exploratory research to define emerging highway safety problems that are poorly understood to highly focused studies on incremental improvements to known safety countermeasures. To encompass this wide range of research activities and to ensure that research is put into practice, a well-structured program should comprise

- Short-term research in support of agency regulatory and programmatic activities,
- Sustained programs of long-term research, and
- Appropriate mechanisms to disseminate the results of the research to managers of highway safety programs and highway system users.

Each of these elements is a necessary component of an effective highway safety research program, but the first two are the primary focus of this study.

Some research capacity will always be needed to support agency rulemaking and programs. In particular, federal agencies with regulatory authority, such as the National Highway Traffic Safety Administration (NHTSA) and the Office of Motor Carriers of the Federal Highway Administration (FHWA), must have the capacity to address specific questions about proposed regulations and to evaluate safety standards that have already been issued so that appropriate changes can be made. Those who are regulated, the automobile manufacturers and the states, must also have the capacity to conduct research to make independent assessments of the costs and benefits of proposed regulations and to support safety improvements they may initiate. The character of this research is generally problem focused and is often short term.

Long-term research is also needed. Although this type of research is applied, that is, conducted with an application in mind, it generally requires several years of sustained study before results are produced. Long-term research requires a long-term perspective, flexible management, and continued financial support to attract and retain talented researchers, encourage innovative approaches, and nurture new ideas through the development phase.

An example of long-term research is the studies on the effects of alcohol on driver performance, which were conducted over several decades (TRB 1987b).[1] The knowledge developed by this research ultimately provided the basis for states to set legal levels of blood alcohol concentration for drivers on the highway and for the development of reliable methods currently used by law enforcement officials to detect alcohol levels in drivers.

Long-term research has been funded by federal agencies and the larger automobile manufacturers. However, it is highly susceptible to budget cutbacks and to the short-term time horizons of agency heads, because the payoffs of this type of research are not realized immediately. When budgets are limited and political time horizons short, the pressures are for short-term gains, and the casualty is often long-term programs of research.

Finally, if the payoffs of research are to be achieved, the findings of research must be put into practice. In some cases the audience is well defined and receptive. Research on improving the design of barrier systems might fall into this category; the user is technically trained and the results can readily be incorporated into engineering practice. In other cases, however, the task is to reach a more general audience and this requires providing the information in a form that is accessible to the general public. For example, if older drivers are to become more aware of the effects of aging on driver performance and crash risk, this information must be presented in practical terms that will reach this target group and provide reasonable guidance (e.g., which types of driving situations present the highest risks, what alternatives are available), so that the audience will heed the information.

GAPS IN CURRENT RESEARCH

The most pressing need identified by the members of the study committee is to provide a more balanced portfolio of short- and long-term research. The cutbacks in funding of the past decade, the elimination of some programs of research, and the narrowing in scope of others have reduced the capacity—both in terms of people and resources—to undertake the long-term research that was described in the preceding section. The following examples illustrate one effect of the neglect of this type of research—the potential for wasting funds and losing opportunities for safety gains that result when the federal government and automobile manufacturers have to make complex decisions without sufficient understanding of the consequences. The decisions involve millions of dollars in highway investments and in vehicle design and engineering improvements to meet regulatory standards.

Unknown Safety Benefits

Technology is moving rapidly to create a host of new informational devices for the driver both in the vehicle and on the highway, but little is known about their effect on driver safety. Head-up displays will provide drivers with essential information, such as vehicle speed, within the driver's field of vision. Navigational systems will provide information on traffic conditions and suggest alternative routes. Changeable-message signs will provide up-to-the-minute information about highway conditions. Providing the driver with more current information about traffic conditions and alerting the driver to potential problems ahead of time could help reduce the problem of driver error, particularly the problem of driver inattention, which has been identified as an important factor contributing to motor vehicle crashes (Malliaris et al. 1983).[2]

Too much information, however, could distract or overload the driver. This could be a particular problem for the older driver, who tends to process information more slowly than the younger one (Staplin et al. 1987). Federal funding of approximately $1 million in human factors research (estimate provided by NHTSA and FHWA) is inadequate to determine how drivers would react to these new technologies and what their net effect would be on safety. Without a more adequate research program, the development, design, and regulation of these technologies are likely to proceed without the full benefit of this information.[3]

Large Implementation Costs

NHTSA will soon enact final regulations for occupant protection in side-impact crashes. Industry is critical of the injury criteria and side-impact dummy that NHTSA has proposed and maintains that the safety benefits projected by the agency are optimistic (Viano et al. 1989a, 1989b). The debate hinges on different views of how injuries occur in side-impact crashes. NHTSA is proposing a standard that is largely based on the skeletal tolerance to the rapid acceleration that occurs in frontal crashes (*Federal Register* 1988).[4]

Industry researchers contend that survivable injuries from side impacts are a function of protecting soft organs, such as the liver and spleen, which have no known injury tolerance relationship with the proposed acceleration standard (Viano et al. 1989a, 1989b). The issue is further complicated by the overrepresentation of older drivers in side-impact crashes (Viano et al. 1990, 181; TRB 1988, 48); little information is available on tolerance to injuries of various types across age groups (Mackay 1988).

NHTSA's proposed regulation to improve side-impact protection could cost as much as $100 per new car or more than $1 billion annually (*Federal Register* 1988, 2,247). Because biomechanics research has not received the level of funding that would support the necessary studies and testing to resolve these issues, it is likely that these and perhaps other regulations, and the large costs they impose on the automobile manufacturers and consumers, will go forward without a more complete understanding of their safety benefits or possible disbenefits.

Lost Opportunities

Over the next several decades, major portions of the nation's highway network will require rehabilitation or reconstruction as they reach the end of their design lives, providing a unique opportunity for incorporating safety improvements as part of highway rebuilding projects. However, a recent study (TRB 1987a) found that many states pay little attention to opportunities for improving safety in designing projects.

Despite nearly half a century of building highways to modern standards, relatively little is known about the safety consequences of design improvements (i.e., to what extent these improvements reduce crashes) or of traffic engineering decisions such as the installation of traffic control devices and the location of signs (TRB 1987a, 77; Hauer 1988a, 249). The information that is available in policy design guidelines and traffic codes rarely provides adequate documentation and quantification of the associated costs and benefits of specific improvements or packages of improvements so that highway designers and traffic engineers can readily analyze alternatives (TRB 1987a, 77). The absence of this information can lead to costly investment decisions, particularly where geometric improvements are involved,[5] that may not yield safety benefits commensurate with the costs. More likely, engineers will miss opportunities for safety improvements.

The foregoing examples underscore the importance of sustained programs of long-term research. The research that could and should form the basis for these complex decisions must be performed well in advance to provide an adequate technical assessment of the issues in a timely manner. Given the complexity of many of these issues, developing this knowledge requires sustained funding over many years. The investment should save many times its costs, however, in avoiding regulations that are not fully effective and in promoting those safety requirements with a high potential for saving lives and reducing injuries.

EMERGING PROBLEMS AND TOPICS FOR RESEARCH

If the safety community is to take the lead in addressing the emerging safety problems associated with a changing travel environment, developing the knowledge base to address these problems should be an immediate priority. Research is only the first step in a lengthy process. The findings of the research must be implemented and only then are the full safety benefits likely to be realized.

Changes are expected in each of the areas affecting highway safety—the human, the vehicle, and the highway—as well as in a fourth area, technology. In Table 3-1 the issues of concern are given for each area, the magnitude and type of problems that are likely to be created are identified, and examples of research topics that could enhance current understanding of the issues are provided.

Older Drivers and Pedestrians

The "graying of America" will continue over the next several decades until it reaches its peak in about 2030 when roughly one-fifth of the

TABLE 3-1   RESEARCH AGENDA TO ADDRESS EMERGING SAFETY PROBLEMS

Changes in Future System Characteristics	Problems Created by Change	Examples of Needed Research
Older drivers and pedestrians	Increase in fatalities and injuries for drivers and pedestrians 65 years and older	Injury tolerance for older persons to improve crash survivability Performance capabilities of older drivers and pedestrians Highway design for older drivers and pedestrians Licensing screening and standards for older drivers Acute care and rehabilitation for elderly crash victims New technologies to aid older drivers
Vehicles Growth of large-truck traffic	Increases in fatalities from large-truck-involved crashes	Performance capabilities of commercial drivers Highway design for large trucks Evaluation of major truck safety programs Police capabilities to detect truck safety violations Truck safety data
Trend toward smaller cars, greater use of light trucks and minivans for personal use	Higher crash risk of smaller vehicles Increased vehicle speed and weight differential, increasing crash risk	Injury reduction through improved occupant protection Enhanced vehicle conspicuity Highway design for a mixed fleet Safety impacts of environmental regulations New technologies for collision avoidance
Increased congestion	Increased potential for vehicle conflicts Increases in injuries and property damage	Behavioral effects of congestion Safety impacts of congestion-related highway design improvements Enforcement methods for congested highways Emergency access on congested highways New informational technologies
Aging of highway infrastructure	Increase in work-zone crashes Inadequate attention to safety improvements	Safety benefits of alternative design improvements Emergency access in work-zone areas New informational technologies
Development of new technologies for use in the vehicle, on the highway, and for safety program management	Potential driver overload Equipment reliability and privacy issues	Behavioral responses to new technologies Automated technologies for enforcement and safety program management New technologies for emergency access in rural areas

population will be 65 or older. Meeting the mobility needs of this segment of the population will become an increasingly important transportation goal. Currently, the absolute number of deaths among older drivers does not represent a large share of total motor vehicle fatalities relative to those among the alcohol-impaired or the young. However, the high involvement rate of older drivers in crashes (on a mileage-driven basis) is second only to that of drivers under the age of 25 (Figure 1-5); fatalities among older drivers are likely to increase as the share of the older driver population rises.

Older pedestrians may become an even greater problem. Pedestrian fatalities for those 75 and older are likely to emerge as the single largest pedestrian problem (Figure 1-7). Compounding these problems is the physical vulnerability of the old, which increases their risk of injury and reduces their likelihood of survival when they are involved in a crash.

The current highway travel environment is not well adapted to the problems of older drivers and pedestrians. Cars and occupant restraints are not designed with the frailty of older persons in mind; highway design standards and roadway signs and markings do not account for the poorer vision of older people and their slower decision-reaction times; and licensing officials lack valid screening procedures to identify those older drivers, or those drivers of any age group, who are at higher risk of crash involvement.

The knowledge to address these problems is inadequate. Little research has been conducted on how much more vulnerable to injury older persons are, how much more time they need to make decisions in traffic, and how to correlate poorer health or driving performance with future crash risk. Developing this knowledge requires a broad program of research, including the following elements.

Injury Tolerance

Current industry design practices and standards for crash protection do not recognize variability in tolerance of different subgroups of the population to impacts experienced in a crash (Mackay 1988, 189). The current standards were developed for the 50th-percentile man. As the population continues to age over the next few decades, it will be increasingly important to understand and quantify how specific age groups, particularly the elderly, differ in tolerance to injury and how these differences vary by the types of crashes in which they tend to be involved. For example, there are substantial age-related differences in the ability of the human frame to tolerate blunt impacts, which are experienced in virtually all motor vehicle crashes. An impact load in a severe collision by a standard safety belt may produce a single rib fracture in a healthy 25-year-old man; the same impact in a 65-year-old may well generate multiple life-threatening fractures, often associated with damage to internal organs (Mackay 1988, 174). The gaps in information about injury in side-impact crashes, in which older persons are overrepresented (Viano et al. 1990), were discussed earlier.

Understanding variations in tolerance to impacts has important implications for vehicle and occupant protection design (Horsch 1987; Viano 1987, 221–223; TRB 1989b). For example, designing an instrument panel with sufficient stiffness to distribute the occupant impact force and avert injuries in a relatively small number of high-speed collisions may, in fact, cause injuries to those more vulnerable segments of the population involved in more numerous low-speed crashes (Mackay 1988, 179). Although it may never be possible to optimize vehicle design and occupant restraint systems to protect all segments of the population, understanding these differences should help evaluate vehicle design modifications that would enhance crash protection for more vulnerable older persons (Mackay 1988, 189).

Performance Capabilities

Changes in performance that accompany aging, such as the poorer vision of older people and their slower decision-reaction times, are not well understood. The lack of knowledge is due in part to limited human factors research and in part to an almost complete absence of attention to the variation in performance across age groups in highway design and traffic operation.

Many standards for highway design and traffic operations assume a performance level that 85 or 95 percent of the population can exceed (McGee et al. 1983). Current assumptions about perception-reaction time and visual acuity, which guide intersection design and sign letter height, are not compatible with the capability of older drivers, particularly in urban traffic (TRB 1988). Considerable evidence shows that older persons have poorer corrected static visual acuity than the rest of the population; such acuity is particularly critical during low illumination conditions. Older persons also make complex decisions more slowly (TRB 1988).

Better estimates should be developed of the performance distribution across age groups on tasks fundamental to highway design and traffic operation, such as perception-brake reaction time, perception time for intersection sight distance, and walking speeds for signal timing.

Much past human factors research has suffered from the use of small samples of subjects who are not representative of the age distribution.

Research projects should be designed to use larger samples that adequately represent older persons.

The decline in performance capabilities of older drivers may be exacerbated by use of prescription drugs, some of which impair performance. Although the elderly represent only 11 percent of the population, they purchase 25 percent of prescription and over-the-counter drugs (McKnight 1988, 109). Laboratory tests have found that over-the-counter prescription drugs like valium and antihistamines impair driving-related performance (Compton 1988, 38). Additional research is needed to determine the nature and extent of the impairment at different dosage levels so that, at a minimum, appropriate warnings can be provided for the driver-user or drugs with less impairing side effects can be prescribed.

Highway Design

Once the performance of older drivers and pedestrians is better understood, the assumptions that underlie many highway design and traffic engineering guidelines should be reevaluated. For example, a performance standard could be developed for highway and street signs based on the degree to which a sign ensures the minimum required visibility distance of older drivers (TRB 1988, 78). Similarly, the level of retroreflectivity needed to provide adequate conspicuity of signing for older drivers could be identified (TRB 1988, 79).

Traffic controls at intersections are another promising area for study, particularly with respect to the problem of older pedestrians. The *Manual on Uniform Traffic Control Devices* assumes a walking speed of 4 ft per second in signal timing; however, a review of the literature found that as much as 30 percent of pedestrians, many of whom are older, walk more slowly (McGee et al. 1983). Nearly half the pedestrian fatalities of those 65 and older occur at intersections without any traffic controls, but little is known about the safety implications of various forms of controls at intersections (Hauer 1988b, 225).

Once the research has been conducted on how current highway and traffic design standards would have to be modified to accommodate the capabilities of older drivers and pedestrians, considerable benefit-cost analysis will be needed. Expected safety benefits, which are likely to extend to other driver and pedestrian age groups, should be weighed against the relevant costs, such as increased traffic congestion from installing traffic controls or increased costs from retrofitting highway geometric design features to accommodate the elderly, to determine where safety improvements are warranted.

Licensing Screening and Standards

More study of both the visual and the cognitive changes associated with aging as they affect driver licensing is warranted. In the area of vision, for example, an improved driver vision screening procedure that measured night vision, peripheral vision, or dynamic visual acuity would better predict future driving performance than current procedures (Waller 1988, 74). For this research to prove useful, however, more thought must be given to how this knowledge can result in practical corrective actions.

Research can also provide the basis for developing valid methods of screening the cognitive performance of drivers, at least to screen for major degradation in cognitive performance such as occurs with the onset of dementia. Older drivers with Alzheimer's disease are at a high risk of crash involvement, but no procedures are available to detect the early onset of this disease (TRB 1988, 60).

Finally, research can help identify appropriate strategies for monitoring older driver performance, introducing licensing restrictions where they are warranted (i.e., graduated driving reduction programs for older drivers), and developing driver-retraining programs aimed at the specific problems of the older driver (Waller 1988).

Acute Care and Rehabilitation

Because of their frailness, the elderly when compared with their younger counterparts not only are more vulnerable to injury in motor vehicle crashes (MacKay 1988) but also have higher mortality rates, longer recovery periods, and higher treatment costs. In a major study of trauma patients treated at over 100 hospitals across the country, the percent of deaths (20.7) among elderly crash victims (i.e., 65 and older) was over twice that for younger victims (Champion et al. 1989). Significant differences in case fatality rates remained after injury severity was controlled for. This study also documented higher complication rates and longer hospital stays among the elderly. In the aggregate, the elderly consume a disproportionate share of the trauma care dollar. In 1985 the elderly represented only 12 percent of the population, but were responsible for 25 percent of all acute care hospitalizations for trauma (MacKenzie et al. 1990). Seventy-two percent of the direct costs for elderly care are paid for by public sources, mainly Medicare (Rice et al. 1989, 89).

Despite these differences in vulnerability and need for trauma care, few studies have focused on the special needs of the elderly for acute care and rehabilitation. Yet recent work has suggested that the identification and treatment of severe trauma in the elderly cannot rely solely on lessons learned from the broader experience in managing younger patients (Champion et al. 1989; Scalea et al. 1990). In particular, more research is needed on the special acute care needs of elderly crash victims. Such research must also examine current problems in financing trauma care systems, such as inadequate reimbursement policies and increasing numbers of uninsured persons, that are threatening the very existence of these centers (Champion and Mabee 1990). In addition, it is important to look at the long-term consequences of motor vehicle injury among the elderly and to identify strategies for optimizing functional capacity, independent living, and quality of life following trauma. Although there is considerable literature that has examined these issues for the elderly who fall and sustain hip fractures (Jette et al. 1987), few studies have looked at recovery following motor vehicle injury in the elderly.

New Technologies

New technologies are being developed that could simplify the driving task and help compensate for the reduced skills of older drivers. Vehicle control systems are likely to become more automated. Antilock brakes are already available on some passenger cars and other technologies are being developed such as smart cruise control, which would automatically warn the driver or slow the vehicle when the gap between vehicles narrows to a preset interval. Warning systems that would alert the driver to unsafe conditions, such as the presence of objects in driver blind spots, or of unsafe proximity to other vehicles (i.e., radar collision avoidance systems) are in the experimental phase but continue to have problems with reliability. Visual enhancement systems, using infrared technology, that would improve driver visibility, particularly at night, are also being tested (TRB 1988, 110).

New driver information technologies, like head-up displays and navigational systems, are already appearing on some vehicle models. Although the purpose of these technologies is to enhance driver awareness of traffic and highway conditions, poorly designed systems may overload driver capacity to accept and process the additional information without distraction. More attention should be given to the slower information-processing capabilities of the older driver in designing these technologies.

Large Trucks

The traveling public is likely to see both more trucks and larger trucks on the highways over the next several decades. Combination truck traffic is projected to grow at an average annual rate of 3.3 percent over the next several decades (Highway Performance Monitoring System data base, special computer run), well above the 2.34 average annual growth rate projected for traffic of all types (U.S. Congress. House. 1989a, 90).

Combination vehicles are also becoming larger. The trucking industry and shippers have adopted the larger equipment authorized by the Surface Transportation Assistance Act of 1982 [trailers up to 48 ft long in a tractor-semitrailer combination and up to 28 ft each in a twin trailer combination (TRB 1989a, 1)]. The majority of states have now passed legislation allowing trailer lengths of 53 ft in tractor-semitrailer combinations (TRB 1989a, 25). Although not all commercial haulers can take advantage of the larger equipment because of weight restrictions, larger equipment has been, and will continue to be, adopted by many carriers.

What are the safety consequences of more trucks on the highways? Drivers of large commercial trucks are about 50 percent less likely to be involved in a crash (on a mileage-driven basis) than drivers of automobiles, but crashes between large trucks and cars are more likely to involve a fatality or serious injury than a crash involving only cars (TRB 1989a). In 1988 passenger cars were involved in roughly 2.6 fatal crashes per 100 million vehicle miles of travel (VMT); combination trucks were involved in 5.0 fatal crashes per 100 million VMT (NHTSA 1989a, 6-14, 6-32; FHWA 1989, 172). Nearly 4,000 fatal crashes involving large trucks (trucks with an unloaded weight of 26,000 lb or more) occur each year;[6] in nearly 85 percent of these crashes the occupant of the involved automobile or motorcycle, or the involved pedestrian or bicyclist is fatally injured rather than the truck driver (NHTSA 1989a, 6-32, 6-34). With more trucks on the highways, the risk of crashes involving fatalities and injuries is likely to increase with exposure levels.

The safety consequences of larger truck sizes are more difficult to establish. A recent review of the literature on the relationship between truck size and safety prepared for a study on truck access found that truck configuration is less important in determining relative crash risk than are the types of roads on which these vehicles travel and the environments in which they operate (TRB 1989a, 122).[7]

Considerable research has been conducted on the safety of large trucks. However, a more concentrated research effort in at least four areas should help advance the knowledge base and learn from what is already known.

Performance Capabilities of Commercial Drivers

Because of the severity of crashes between large trucks and cars, and the delays caused by truck crashes on congested roads, research to ensure the high performance of truck drivers is a major priority. Steps are being taken to improve truck driver performance. Blood alcohol standards for commercial truck and bus drivers are being reduced, in recognition of the special demands of driving heavy vehicles and the special risks to passenger vehicle occupants involved in truck crashes (TRB 1987b). In addition, the federal government and the states are devoting new attention to commercial driver licensing and vehicle inspections.

However, field research and driver surveys indicate that some commercial drivers abuse amphetamines and marijuana (Lund et al. 1987; Beilock and Capelle 1987). A recent study of heavy-truck crashes in which the truck driver was fatally injured found that one-third of these drivers tested positive for alcohol and other drugs of abuse (NTSB 1990, v). Marijuana and alcohol were the most prevalent drugs found in toxicological tests of fatally injured drivers; stimulants were the most frequently identified drug class among this same group of fatally injured truck drivers (NTSB 1990, v). More needs to be known about the extent of drug use in the general population of truck drivers and the effects of these drugs on driving performance, particularly in combination with fatigue. FHWA is just beginning a major research program to address driver fatigue through on-the-road tests and surveys (Schulz 1989, 21). The purposes of the research are to understand the extent of the problem, develop appropriate countermeasures, and provide a sound basis for possible revisions in hours-of-service rules for drivers (Schulz 1989, 21). In addition, research can help devise better methods for screening drivers suspected by investigating officers of being impaired by drugs and develop better countermeasures to deter drug use by commercial drivers.

Highway Design for Large Trucks

The choice of design vehicle is critical to many geometric design guidelines used by highway engineers, such as sight distance requirements for passing and stopping and provision of adequate turning radii at curves, intersections, and ramps to prevent vehicles from encroaching on opposing traffic lanes or running off the road. Large trucks are often the most critical design vehicle, yet it took 8 years before the longer truck trailer lengths that were authorized by the Surface Transportation Assistance Act of 1982 were incorporated in the 1990 edition of the American Association of State Highway and Transportation Officials (AASHTO) geometric policy guide—a process that should be expedited (TRB 1989a, 128).[8] Because they need access to shippers, many large trucks may travel roads and negotiate intersections that have not been built to even current AASHTO design standards. Although some research is in progress

(Harwood et al. 1990), more is needed on the performance and handling capabilities of large trucks in relation to the design features of existing roads to assess the impacts on safety of additional large-truck traffic and where safety appears to be compromised, to suggest where truck volumes are sufficient to warrant upgrading.

Evaluation of Major Truck Safety Programs

Several new safety initiatives for commercial motor vehicles were introduced during the 1980s: the Motor Carrier Safety Assistance Program, which provides for frequent inspection of trucks and buses; the Safety Review Program, which evaluates carriers' compliance with safety regulations; and most recently, the Commercial Drivers License Program, which requires that commercial drivers hold a single license and provides minimum standards for state testing and licensing of commercial drivers (U.S. Congress. Senate. 1989a, 4–5, 13). Although some evaluations have been conducted of the first two programs,[9] provision should be made to evaluate the last, which is the nation's largest driver-licensing initiative. This program represents a large commitment of state resources, albeit in response to federal requirements. The data system being developed for state sharing of information on commercial drivers could provide the basis for greater sharing of information on the general driving population.

Police Capabilities To Detect Truck Safety Violations

Truck safety violations, such as driving with poorly maintained or misadjusted brakes or driving overweight, have the potential for creating a far greater hazard in a truck than in a passenger vehicle because of the adverse effects of the greater size and weight of the truck in the event of a crash. Many safety violations, however, are difficult to detect in a truck moving in traffic. Furthermore, except for state highway patrols, police officers receive relatively little training in detecting and enforcing truck safety violations. Fortunately, new technologies, such as weigh-in-motion equipment, which automatically measures vehicle axle weights while the vehicle is in motion, have been developed to enhance police detection capabilities.

Research is needed to determine what combination of enforcement strategies and technology will maximize police capabilities to deter and remove unsafe trucks from the highways. Specific research issues include determining the type and extent of training required for local police (i.e., enough training to detect significant problems, yet brief enough in duration to be practical), and examining the costs and benefits of emerging and available technologies that can enhance police detection abilities.

Truck Safety Data

Existing truck safety data are inadequate to determine the magnitude and trends of truck safety problems and to guide actions to reduce crash losses. A forthcoming study on truck safety data needs by the Transportation Research Board found, for example, that truck travel data by type of truck and by geographic area are not consistently or frequently collected (TRB 1990). Such data are critical to the calculation of crash rates for monitoring the performance of different truck types. As a first priority, the study recommends development of a National Monitoring System, which would assemble nationwide crash and travel data for medium and heavy trucks (i.e., for trucks with a gross vehicle weight over 10,000 lb) on a uniform and frequent basis. Follow-up study is likely to be necessary to ensure that critical data gaps are closed.

Additional research is also needed to identify methods for improving the efficiency and reliability of data collection. Portable computerized data input devices would allow immediate paperless accident data entry from the field, presumably improving the accuracy and speed of accident reporting. Field data could also be augmented by video records of the accident scene. Satellite technology could facilitate the recording of accurate locational data—route, milepost—on accident reports. Automated devices are in use in most states to provide traffic count data (Grenzeback et al. 1988, 32) and more sophisticated systems are available that can distinguish vehicle types, including different truck configurations, and even track the location of vehicles en route (Grenzeback et al. 1988, 2). Many of these measures would have benefits that extend beyond monitoring truck safety to the entire passenger fleet. Research can help sort through the costs and benefits of alternative technologies and determine where they can be most effectively deployed.

Vehicle Mix

In the next few decades, drivers are likely to experience an even greater mix of vehicles on the highway than today. The projected growth in large-truck traffic was discussed in the preceding section. Light trucks are being used increasingly for personal travel; they now represent nearly one-third of new-car retail sales in the United States and this share is likely to increase (MVMA 1989, 16, 19). Passenger vehicles have been getting lighter and smaller.[10] Because of continued environmental and energy concerns, these trends are not likely to be reversed in the near future.

The growing disparity in vehicle size and weight is likely to have at least two adverse effects on safety. First, differences in vehicle size and weight produce performance differences that can introduce variance in the traffic flow and increase crash risk. The most obvious example is large trucks. Their greater weight results in poorer accelerating and braking capabilities than passenger vehicles, with the effect that they may often travel at lower speeds than the prevailing traffic. It is known that variation in speed among different vehicles generally increases passing maneuvers and braking, thereby generating more potential for vehicle conflict and increasing crash risk (Solomon 1964).

Second, in the event of a crash, the degree of protection afforded vehicle occupants and nonoccupants differs greatly by the size and weight of the involved vehicles. For example, passenger vehicle occupants are highly vulnerable in truck-involved crashes. However, even the difference in weight between a large and a small car can have a significant effect on injury severity in a crash.[11]

Addressing the potential adverse effects on safety from a more diverse mix of vehicles on the highway requires research in at least five areas.

Improved Occupant Protection

Effective methods for mitigating injury through protective devices, such as safety belts and other restraint systems, are well known but not always widely used. Because of the need for increased protection in a mixed-fleet environment, research on the most efficient and cost-effective means of increasing voluntary restraint use was identified as "one of the most urgent research needs" in a recent report on occupant restraint systems (TRB 1989b). As of 1990, 36 states and the District of Columbia had mandatory safety belt use laws, but about half of the vehicle occupants in these states continue to ignore the law (TRB 1989b, 7-8). Although automatic or passive restraints are now required on all passenger vehicles and will be required for light trucks,[12] it will be 15 years or more before these systems are available in 90 percent of the automobile fleet and longer for light trucks (TRB 1989b, 7).

Enhanced Vehicle Conspicuity

Enhancing the conspicuity of vehicles, particularly of vehicles that are likely to move more slowly than the average traffic, can help avoid crashes. Better methods of illuminating the sides and rear of large trucks are being investigated to help avoid rear-end collisions with faster-moving passenger vehicles at night. Unloaded flatbed trucks are a particular problem because of their poor visibility to approaching motorists.

Highway Design

Although highways are designed to handle a mix of vehicle types, accommodating vehicles of different performance characteristics is difficult. Large trucks can block road signs for small passenger vehicles, and roadside hardware that has been designed to accommodate passenger vehicles and light trucks is not effective for heavy trucks. For example, crash attenuators, which are used at points where fixed objects cannot be removed, will safely decelerate vehicles as heavy as 4,500 lb, but they will not work for 80,000-lb vehicles (TRB 1989a, 140). Similarly, most roadside barriers, including guardrails, concrete median barriers, and bridge rails, will safely contain and redirect passenger vehicles but not heavy trucks with high centers of gravity (TRB 1989a, 140). Some innovative barrier designs have been created for large trucks, but their cost is prohibitive except at critical locations (Hirsch 1986). More research is needed on design options that can accommodate a range of vehicle types and where they can be deployed cost-effectively.

One strategy for addressing the problems created by a wide mix of vehicles on the highway is to separate the traffic by vehicle type, thereby reducing the potential for conflict between vehicles of different performance characteristics. For example, numerous proposals have advocated restricting trucks to specific lanes on multilane highways, putting time-of-day restrictions on truck travel, or constructing separate truck lanes in certain corridors. A recent study of proposed lane restrictions for large trucks found that keeping large trucks in the right lane, in combination with a lower speed limit for the trucks, actually increased crash risk (Garber and Gadiraju 1989, 2). Other options, such as time-of-day restrictions and separate truck lanes, involve substantial costs. More study of the costs and benefits of alternative approaches would help develop sensible policies.

Safety Impacts of Environmental Regulations

The trend toward lighter and smaller passenger vehicles is in part the product of environmental regulations to improve air quality and conserve energy. Environmental and energy goals, however, may be achieved at the expense of safety, because smaller, lighter cars afford vehicle occupants less protection from death and injury in the event of a crash (Graham and Crandall 1989; Partyka and Boehly 1989). The trade-offs among highway safety, clean air, and energy efficiency would make a timely issue for study, because Congress is considering legislation that would require automobile manufacturers to significantly improve corporate average fuel economy (CAFE) standards on new cars (Brown 1990, H-1).

New Technologies for Collision Avoidance

Another way to reduce the adverse effects on safety of a diverse mix of vehicles on the road is to reduce the potential for conflict by advanced systems of vehicle communication and control. For a description of relevant research topics, see the discussion under the subhead New Technology.

Congestion

Traffic is growing at a much faster pace than highway capacity, with the result that drivers are likely to be traveling on increasingly congested highways in the next several decades. With more vehicles on the road, the potential for vehicle conflicts and multivehicle collisions increases (Hall and Pendleton 1989, 17). However, crash severity will depend on the amount of congestion, which affects the speed of the traffic. In very congested conditions, crashes may result in injuries and property damage but fewer fatalities than in less congested conditions where vehicle speeds are higher. More study is needed on a wide range of issues concerning the safety impacts of congestion.

Behavioral Effects

Congested highways may affect driver behavior in ways that have an adverse impact on safety. Increased driver disregard of traffic control devices (i.e., running red lights, failing to stop at stop signs), increased risk taking (i.e., driving too close, lane weaving), and episodes of violence (e.g., the shootings on the congested freeways of southern California) may, in part, be attributed to the stress and frustration of driving under congested traffic conditions (Deacon 1988, 20). However, the extent of these behaviors and their total impact on safety are not well known. Congested driving conditions also require vigilant driver behavior; attentional lapses can precipitate a crash. With increased congestion likely, more in-depth study of the extent to which traffic congestion increases the stress of driving, attentional requirements, and the extent of risk taking and how these affect crash risk under varying levels of congestion has high priority (Deacon 1988, 20).

Highway Design Improvements

A related area for study is the safety impacts of design changes that are being implemented to relieve urban traffic congestion. Because it is difficult to construct major new highways in built-up areas, low-cost capacity improvements are being made by reducing lane, shoulder, and median width on existing roads. The potential of these capacity-enhancing measures for increasing lane encroachment or conflict in merging situations as well as their effect under special conditions, such as high speeds, curving alignments, and substantial truck traffic, are largely unknown and form timely topics for investigation (Deacon 1988, 19; TRB 1989c, 3–4). Recent research by Harwood (1990) has begun to address these topics by comparing the advantages and disadvantages of design alternatives for urban arterial streets, such as reducing lane width and installing left turn lanes, on their operational and safety performance.

Enforcement Methods

Growing congestion is likely to increase the difficulty of traditional methods of law enforcement. On a crowded highway, pulling violators over for ticketing may create a hazard or may simply be impossible if shoulder space is converted into a traffic lane during peak periods. New automated enforcement techniques are being developed to alleviate these problems. For a discussion of relevant research topics, see the section headed New Technology.

Emergency Access

More congestion is likely to increase the time and difficulty of reaching crash victims at the crash site. Low-cost measures to alleviate traffic congestion, such as narrowing lanes and using shoulders as traffic lanes in peak periods, could exacerbate the problem of access for emergency vehicles. More thorough analyses of the safety implications of congestion-reducing measures for emergency access as well as alternative methods (e.g., by helicopter) and costs of obtaining access should be conducted.

New Informational Technologies

Advanced driver information systems have the potential to assist the driver in safely handling the complexity of the traffic environment, particularly under congested conditions. For example, with road-to-vehicle communications, the driver could be advised to begin slowing well in advance of traffic stopped by congestion or a crash. Vehicle-to-vehicle communication, through a radar collision avoidance system, could provide an even more sophisticated means of alerting drivers of impending danger in time for them to take corrective action. More study is needed on the design of these systems to keep them from distracting the driver and to minimize driver information overload. The costs of alternative technologies and strategies for introducing new technologies on a timely basis are other appropriate topics for research (Deacon 1988, 22).

Aging of the Highway Infrastructure

Major portions of the highway network will require rehabilitation or reconstruction over the next several decades. From a safety perspective, the aging of the highway infrastructure is a two-edged sword. Crash risk is likely to increase in and near construction zone sites as the potential for conflict between drivers and work crews increases. However, rehabilitation of the highway network offers a unique opportunity to upgrade highway safety standards as part of highway rebuilding projects. Research can help make the most of this opportunity as well as mitigate the adverse safety effects of more highway reconstruction.

Alternative Design Improvements

Despite nearly half a century of building highways to modern standards and apparent concern for highway safety in design, relatively little is known about the safety consequences of highway design improvements, that is, to what extent these improvements reduce the severity or frequency of crashes (TRB 1987a, 77). Where information is available, the results are often slow to be incorporated into practice (TRB 1987a, 77; Hauer 1988a, 254).

Research is needed to sort out what is known, what is disputed, and what is unknown about the relationship between safety and roadway design. Because the field is vast, research efforts should be concentrated initially on those design improvements that could be included in reconstruction, resurfacing, restoration, and rehabilitation (4R and 3R) projects because of the opportunity for integrating safety improvements during these projects. A good start has already been made in TRB's recent study of 3R-related design features, which attempted to identify whether a relationship between safety and a design feature exists, what the direction of the relationship is, and what the likely magnitude of the safety impacts is over a range of possible improvements (TRB 1987a, 80). As a follow-on effort, FHWA is undertaking a critical assessment of known relationships between geometric design elements and crashes (personal communication with Chief, Safety Design Division, FHWA, September 13, 1990). More data are needed, not only on the safety benefits of upgrading specific design features, but also on the benefits of alternative packages of improvements, making explicit the trade-offs among them. Quantitative estimates of the safety and cost implications of design policies should be made available in a format that is readily accessible to the practicing design engineer.

Analysis of tort liability claims for defective highway designs could also help target those highway design deficiencies meriting close study. Identification of the most prevalent claims and the distribution of awards could pinpoint those design improvements for which savings from reduced claims would be largest (Wallen 1990, 4; TRB 1989c).

Emergency Access in Work-Zone Areas

Highways under construction may create bottlenecks for emergency access vehicles attempting to reach crash victims near or at construction-zone sites. Alternative methods of providing for emergency access should be considered in the design and setup of construction work zones and the costs and benefits of alternative strategies for obtaining access should be examined.

New Informational Technologies

Advanced driver information systems have the potential to warn drivers well in advance of impending hazardous situations, such as traffic rerouting at a construction zone. Although signs currently warn drivers to slow before reaching a construction-zone site, these warnings are often ignored. An information system that provides drivers with real-time assessments of slowdowns or bottlenecks in construction areas and alternative routing advisories is more likely to be heeded, and could alleviate congested and dangerous driving conditions in the immediate vicinity of these areas. More study is needed on system design to reduce the potential for driver overload and distraction and on the costs of alternative technologies.

New Technology

Advances in electronics and communications technology are likely to transform the vehicle and the highway of the future. These technologies are being developed for the general driving population, although the changes may adversely affect certain groups, such as older drivers, more than others. The primary purpose of many of the improvements that will be part of an intelligent vehicle-highway system, such as vehicle navigational systems and automated vehicle control, is the reduction of urban congestion, but they also have potential for improving highway safety.

To date, limited research has been conducted on these technologies from a safety perspective. If their design and development proceed without adequate attention to driver capabilities and limitations, the full safety potential of these systems may not be realized; poorly designed systems could actually degrade safety. A broad program of human factors research should be initiated soon if the findings are to influence the design of these new technologies.

New technologies are also likely to transform current enforcement practices, licensing procedures, and motor vehicle inspections, increasing the efficiency and reliability of detecting undesirable driving behavior, screening for driving skills, and testing vehicle condition. They may also provide an opportunity for improving emergency access, particularly in rural areas. Promising topics for research exist in all these areas.

Behavioral Responses

A substantially expanded program of human factors research would advance knowledge about the effects of new vehicle technologies on driver behavior. The driving task involves continuous receipt of information, information evaluation, and timely decision making. New advanced information systems have the potential to provide drivers with substantially more data on highway and traffic conditions than they currently receive. But do drivers have the capability to accept and process the additional information without overload or distraction? And how will their reactions vary by age, fatigue level, extent of impairment from alcohol and drug use, and situation (i.e., emergency conditions)?

Driver responses to advanced vehicle control systems, such as smart cruise control and radar braking, raise somewhat different concerns. Here issues of driver acceptance of surrendering a measure of control of the vehicle to automated systems and the related effects on driver vigilance and risk taking should be examined.

New technology could also enhance the research effort itself. The U.S. Department of Transportation believes that a state-of-the-art driving simulator, which would allow researchers to study driver responses to specific vehicle systems in a safe, dynamic, controllable, and realistic environment, is crucial to this effort. Such a simulator is estimated to cost between $20 million and $30 million, with projected annual operating costs of approximately $4 million (U.S. Congress. House. 1989a, 1,000). Many researchers fear that a simulator would never approximate real-life conditions and would drain scarce resources for research. An independent feasibility study is needed to determine which tasks could be handled only by a state-of-the-art simulator, how crucial these are to research priorities, and what alternatives are available. NHTSA will soon embark on a needs assessment that will address many of these issues (personal communication with Director, Office of Crash Avoidance, Feb. 2, 1990).

Enforcement and Safety Program Management

Resource constraints and congested traffic conditions are limiting traditional law enforcement strategies that rely on police detection and on-the-road apprehension of aberrant or illegal driving behavior. Yet public compliance with traffic laws rests in part on a visible and credible level of enforcement. New automated technologies are being developed that can increase the efficiency of enforcement as well as the probability of apprehension. For example, devices have been developed and are being used to measure automatically the speed of a vehicle and to photograph the license plate of a violator. The vehicle owner is then mailed a traffic citation. An emerging technology that could aid enforcement is a visible driver's license (perhaps also an audible license emitted by a radio signal). As highways and vehicles become increasingly sophisticated, with advanced guidance and communications electronics, the opportunities for automated enforcement will grow.

These technologies can be (and are being) proven technically, but more needs to be known about their effectiveness in deterring dangerous driving behavior and their acceptability to the police and the public. Automatic speed-monitoring devices, for example, generate storms of angry letters to the editor when proposed, but a public opinion survey in the two communities where they are being used in the United States found that despite the strong opposition of a minority, most residents supported their use (Freedman et al. 1989). The growing application of video cameras and computer technologies to ease traffic congestion will provide further opportunities to test public opinion about their use in traffic law enforcement and to measure their effectiveness in reducing speeding.

New technologies also have potential for streamlining labor-intensive licensing procedures and motor vehicle inspection programs, but the capital costs and benefits of automated methods and the obstacles to their introduction have received limited attention. Personal computers and video disk technology could be used increasingly in devising methods for screening candidate drivers for driving knowledge, vision, and skill performance. Part-task driving simulators could also be developed to measure certain driver performance characteristics, such as perception-reaction times, that could be unsafe to test on the road and to examine important perceptual aspects of driving, which depend on highway and traffic conditions that cannot be caused to occur on the road. Research is needed to determine which testing procedures are candidates for automation and the cost-effectiveness of alternative testing methods.

New technologies could also revolutionize the way that current motor vehicle inspections are conducted. As in-vehicle diagnostic systems become more common, time-consuming vehicle inspection procedures, such as removing wheels to test the brakes, may become unnecessary (NHTSA 1989b, 56). Moreover, as diagnostic equipment becomes more automated, vehicle inspection methods should also become less dependent on subjective assessments and potentially inconsistent procedures of inspection personnel, increasing public confidence in these programs. The job for researchers is to identify which technological improvements are likely to prove cost-effective and how their introduction can be encouraged.

Emergency Access in Rural Areas

Although great strides have been made in improving emergency access and trauma care facilities, particularly in urban areas, many rural areas are not well served. Response times are less than 10 min for 90 percent of urban crashes, but up to twice as long for an equivalent percentage of rural crashes (NHTSA 1989a, 9-7, 9-8). These differences contribute to higher fatal crash rates and a greater number of fatalities on rural roads. New in-vehicle communication devices, such as car phones and two-way radios, provide a means for direct access to emergency systems that could reduce response times. However, if the problems of providing emergency services at affordable costs in rural areas are to be fully addressed, more study is needed of the costs and benefits of expanded coverage of emergency communications systems, such as the widely used 911 system, improved training for first responders, and better coordination of emergency service provision.

SUMMARY THEMES

Promising topics for research identified under each of the expected areas of change in the travel environment (Table 3-1) can be grouped under six broad themes, which are summarized here.

Crash Avoidance Through Better Understanding of Driver and Pedestrian Behavior

Human error, or inappropriate driving behavior, is the major factor contributing to motor vehicle crashes. An expanded program of human factors research could improve understanding of driver attentional and workload capacities and the potential for new on-board diagnostic and warning systems to enhance driver capabilities in an increasingly complex driving environment. Particular attention should be paid to the capabilities and limitations of older drivers and pedestrians and commercial drivers to provide the basis for driver-training programs, license-screening procedures, vehicle design modifications, and highway and traffic design improvements more directly tailored to these high-risk groups.

Occupant Protection in Crashes

Research has led to major improvements in vehicle design that protect occupants in a frontal crash. The protection that these improvements can afford will become increasingly important with the trend toward smaller passenger vehicles and larger trucks. Realizing the full benefits of these improvements requires further study on ways to increase use of highly effective occupant protection devices, such as safety belts.

Further major advances in vehicle crashworthiness require more intensive research in biomechanics. Considerable work has been done on understanding the underlying mechanism of injury and human response to lateral impact forces in side-impact crashes, but more is left to do if this knowledge is to be translated into vehicle design improvements that will produce significant injury reductions. More attention must be paid to variations in tolerance to injury, particularly for vulnerable populations like older drivers and pedestrians if they are to be afforded better protection in crashes.

Highway Safety Design and Operation

The highway network will be handling an increasing number of vehicles, a more diverse vehicle mix, and a changing population of drivers in the coming decades. Major portions of the highways themselves will reach the end of their design lives, creating an opportunity for upgrades and improvements to accommodate changes in the driver and vehicle mix. To take advantage of this opportunity, more needs to be known about the safety effects of alternative highway design and traffic engineering improvements to accommodate a mix of different vehicles (e.g., guardrail and median barrier systems that can deflect large trucks as well as small passenger vehicles), alleviate congestion (e.g., narrowing lane width, converting shoulders to lanes), and address the special problems of an aging population of drivers and pedestrians (e.g., special left-turn lanes, median refuge islands). Once the safety benefits of alternative improvements are better understood, they can be more readily weighed against the costs to determine where improvements can yield net safety benefits.

Postcrash Acute Care and Rehabilitation

Development of emergency medical services and regional trauma care systems over the past 20 years is responsible, in part, for the record of improved survivability from motor vehicle crashes. However, these systems will face new challenges in the decades ahead. The growing number of older drivers and pedestrians, their greater vulnerability to injury, and their longer recovery from trauma will put new demands on acute care and rehabilitation facilities. Research on better ways to handle elderly crash victims at the crash site as well as methods to shorten their postcrash recovery could have substantial payoffs in mitigating crash trauma for the elderly and reducing medical costs. Better methods of providing rapid access to all crash victims, both on congested highways and in rural areas, should also be examined. Further gains in the areas of acute care and rehabilitation must address not only changes in the travel environment, but changes in the health care system as well. Problems in financing trauma care systems, such as inadequate reimbursement policies and increasing numbers of uninsured persons, are threatening the existence of trauma care centers.

Management of Highway Safety

Changes in the travel environment are likely to require modifications in how licensing programs and enforcement activities are conducted. For example, as more becomes known about the capabilities of certain groups of drivers that are likely to be more prevalent on the highways in the future, such as the elderly and commercial drivers, as well as their limitations under certain driving conditions (e.g., at night and while fatigued), this knowledge can be used to devise more appropriate methods for monitoring and screening drivers at the time of licensing and license renewal, and for modifying licensing practices.

Increased highway congestion will likely require changes in the way that enforcement is conducted, at least during peak traffic periods when stopping and ticketing drivers may create a hazard. Growing numbers of trucks on the highways will require more efficient ways of deploying law enforcement personnel to detect truck safety violations. New technologies are being developed with the potential to automate many traditional enforcement activities as well as labor-intensive programs such as driver licensing and motor vehicle inspection. The costs and benefits of these new technologies and the obstacles to their introduction should be further investigated and addressed if their full potential is to be realized.

Driver Information and Vehicle Control Technologies

Technical advances are also being made in driver information and vehicle control systems as part of the development of intelligent vehicle-highway systems. New driver aid systems can warn of potentially hazardous conditions, such as approaching work zones or heavily congested traffic conditions, and possibly automate some functions, such as emergency braking. The technologies have tremendous potential to reduce the risk of collisions from driver inattention and to compensate for reduced driver skills. However, if these benefits are to be realized, much more needs to be learned about how drivers will react to these new systems so that they can be designed to minimize the potential for information overload, distraction, or driver complacency. This research must begin shortly if it is to influence the design of these systems, many of which are moving rapidly to production.

NOTES

1. Actually, research on the effect of alcohol on automobile crashes has been conducted in the United States since the 1930s (TRB 1987b, 40).
2. In a study of passenger vehicles involved in crashes, Malliaris et al. found that nearly half of the involved vehicles were proceeding straight down the road immediately before the crash, suggesting that driver inattention or failure to see may play an important role in crashes.

3. NHTSA has already issued an advance notice of proposed rulemaking on head-up displays (*Federal Register* 1989).
4. The proposed test is similar in concept to the tests used in frontal crashes, which measure acceleration to the head, thorax, and femur of anthropometric test devices (crash dummies). The proposed test (Thoracic Trauma Index) would be based on a measure of acceleration to the left side of the thorax (Eppinger et al. 1984).
5. The costs of making geometric improvements are often large relative to other rehabilitation, restoration, and resurfacing project costs (TRB 1987a, 77).
6. The definition of large or heavy trucks used in NHTSA's Fatal Accident Reporting System differs from the definition used by FHWA. NHTSA defines a heavy truck as a single-unit truck with gross vehicle weight greater than 26,000 lb, a tractor-trailer combination, a truck with cargo trailer or trailers, and/or a truck-tractor pulling no trailer (NHTSA 1989a, glossary).
7. To the extent that larger trucks reduce the number of trips required to haul an equivalent load, larger equipment can improve safety by reducing the total miles of truck travel (TRB 1989a, 122).
8. The 1990 edition includes several new design vehicles, including tractor-semitrailers with 48- and 53-ft trailers. Guidance is provided on how these new design vehicles affect curve and intersection pavement width and intersection sight distance requirements.
9. Two studies were conducted by the Congressional Research Service (U.S. Congress. Senate. 1988, 1989b) and another by the Office of Technology Assessment (OTA 1988).
10. Between 1980 and 1987, the average weight of the on-road car fleet dropped from 3,524 to 3,138 lb (Partyka and Boehly 1989, 77). Thirty percent of all new-car retail sales, not counting imports, are classified as compacts and subcompacts (MVMA 1989, 16).
11. Partyka and Boehly (1989, 77) estimated that the reduction in the average weight of the passenger vehicle fleet between 1980 and 1987 increased the number of moderate injuries to drivers in single-vehicle nonrollover crashes each year by 5.6 percent. Their analysis controlled for such factors as damage type, number of involved vehicles, rollover occurrence, severity of non-rollover crashes, and victim age. Factors such as differences in vehicle wheelbase dimensions were not taken into account.
12. NHTSA recently (January 1990) issued a notice of proposed rulemaking to require airbags or automatic safety belts for pickups, vans, and utility vehicles beginning with the 1994 model year.

REFERENCES

ABBREVIATIONS

DOT	U.S. Department of Transportation
FHWA	Federal Highway Administration
MVMA	Motor Vehicle Manufacturers Association
NCHRP	National Cooperative Highway Research Program
NHTSA	National Highway Traffic Safety Administration
NTSB	National Transportation Safety Board

OTA   Office of Technology Assessment
TRB   Transportation Research Board

Beilock, R., and R. Capelle. 1987. Economic Pressure, Long Distance Trucking, and Safety. *Journal of the Transportation Research Forum,* Vol. 28, No. 1.

Brown, W. 1990. Weighing Mileage and Lives. *The Washington Post,* March 25.

Champion, H.R., W.S. Copes, D. Buyer, M.E. Flanagan, L. Bain, and W.J. Sacco. 1989. Major Trauma in Geriatric Patients. *American Journal of Public Health,* Vol. 79, No. 9, pp. 1278–1282.

Champion, H.R., and M.S. Mabee. 1990. An American Crisis in Trauma Care Reimbursement. *Emergency Care Quarterly,* Vol. 6, No. 2, July, pp. 65–87.

Compton, R. 1988. *Use of Controlled Substances and Highway Safety: A Report to Congress.* Report DOT-HS-807-261. NHTSA, U.S. Department of Transportation, March, 44 pp.

Deacon, J.A. 1988. *Highway Safety Research, Development, and Technology Transfer.* Research Report KTC-88-1. Kentucky Transportation Center, University of Kentucky, Lexington, Aug. 30, 27 pp.

Eppinger, R., J. Marcus, and R. Morgan. 1984. *Development of Dummy and Injury Index for NHTSA's Thoracic Side Impact Protection Program.* SAE Technical Paper Series. 840885. Society of Automotive Engineers, Warrendale, Pa.

Federal Register. 1988. Vol. 53, No. 17, Jan. 27, pp. 2,239–2,254 and 2,254–2,260.

Federal Register. 1989. Vol. 54, No. 236, Dec. 11, pp. 50,783-50,785.

FHWA. 1989. *Highway Statistics 1988.* U.S. Department of Transportation.

Freedman, M., A. Williams, and A. Lund. 1989. *Public Opinion Regarding Photo Radar.* Insurance Institute for Highway Safety, Arlington, Va.

Garber, N.J., and R. Gadiraju. 1989. *The Effect of Truck Traffic Control Strategies on Traffic Flow and Safety on Multilane Highways.* AAA Foundation for Traffic Safety, Washington, D.C., Sept.

Graham, J.D., and R.W. Crandall. 1989. The Effect of Fuel Economy Standards on Automobile Safety. *Journal of Law and Economics,* Vol. 32, No. 1, April, pp. 97–118.

Grenzeback, L.R., J.R. Stowers, and A.B. Boghani. 1988. *NCHRP Report 303: Feasibility of a National Heavy-Vehicle Monitoring System.* TRB, National Research Council, Washington, D.C., Dec., 68 pp.

Hall, J.H., and O.J. Pendleton. 1989. *Relationship Between V/C Ratios and Accident Rates.* Report FHWA-HPR-NM-88-02. University of New Mexico, Albuquerque, June, 23 pp.

Harwood, D.W. 1990. *Effective Utilization of Street Width on Urban Arterials.* NCHRP Report 330. TRB, National Research Council, Washington, D.C., (forthcoming).

Harwood, D.W., J.M. Mason, W.D. Glauz, B.T. Kulakowski, and K. Fitzpatrick. 1990. *Truck Characteristics for Use in Highway Design and Operation,* Volume 1: *Research Report.* Report FHWA-RD-89-226. Midwest Research Institute, Kansas City, Missouri (forthcoming).

Hauer, E. 1988a. A Case for Science-Based Road Safety Design and Management. In *Highway Safety: At the Crossroads* (R.E. Stammer, ed.), American Society of Civil Engineers, New York, N.Y., pp. 241–267.

Hauer, E. 1988b. The Safety of Older Persons at Intersections. In *Special Report 218: Transportation in an Aging Society,* Volume 2, TRB, National Research Council, Washington, D.C., pp. 194–252.

Hirsch, T.J. 1986. Longitudinal Barriers for Buses and Trucks. In *Transportation Research Record 1052,* TRB, National Research Council, Washington, D.C., pp. 95–102.

Horsch, J.D. 1987. *Evaluation of Occupant Protection from Responses Measured in Laboratory Tests.* 870222. Society of Automotive Engineers, Warrendale, Pa.

Jette, A.M., B.A. Harris, P.D. Cleary, and E.W. Campion. 1987. Functional Recovery after Hip Fracture. *Archives of Physical Medicine and Rehabilitation,* Vol. 68, No. 10, pp. 735–740.

Lund, A., D. Preusser, R. Blomberg, and A. Williams. 1987. *Drug Use by Tractor-Trailer Drivers.* Insurance Institute for Highway Safety, Arlington, Va.

Mackay, M. 1988. Crash Protection for Older Persons. In *Special Report 218: Transportation in an Aging Society,* Volume 2, TRB, National Research Council, Washington, D.C., pp. 158–193.

MacKenzie, E.J., J.A. Morris, G.S. Smith, and M. Fahey. 1990. Acute Hospital Costs of Trauma in the United States: Implications for Regionalized Systems of Care. *Journal of Trauma* (in press).

McGee, H.W., K.G. Hooper, W.E. Hughes, and E. Benson. 1983. *Highway Design and Operations Standards Affected by Driver Characteristics: Final Technical Report.* Report FHWA/RD-83-015. FHWA, U.S. Department of Transportation.

McKnight, A.J. 1988. Driver and Pedestrian Training. In *Special Report 218: Transportation in an Aging Society,* Volume 2, TRB, National Research Council, Washington, D.C., pp. 101–133.

Malliaris, A., R. Nicholson, J. Hedlund, and S. Schneider. 1983. *Crash Avoidance Research.* SAE SP-544. Society of Automotive Engineers, Warrendale, Pa.

MVMA. 1989. *Motor Vehicle Facts and Figures '89.* Detroit, Mich.

NHTSA. 1989a. *Fatal Accident Reporting System.* Report DOT-HS-807-507. U.S. Department of Transportation, Dec.

NHTSA. 1989b. *Study of the Effectiveness of State Motor Vehicle Inspection Programs.* Report DOT-HS-807-468. U.S. Department of Transportation, Aug., 91 pp.

NTSB. 1990. *Fatigue, Alcohol, Other Drugs, and Medical Factors in Fatal-to the-Driver Heavy Truck Crashes.* Volume 1. Report NTSB/SS-90/01. Feb., 179 pp.

OTA. 1988. *Gearing Up for Safety.* Report OTA-SET-382. Congress of the United States, Sept., 188 pp.

Partyka, S.C., and W.A. Boehly. 1989. Passenger Car Weight and Injury Severity in Single Vehicle Nonrollover Crashes. In *Papers on Car Size—Safety and Trends,* Report DOT-HS-807-444, NHTSA, U.S. Department of Transportation, June, pp. 73–107.

Rice, D.P., E.J. MacKenzie, and Associates. 1989. *Cost of Injury in the United States: A Report to Congress.* Institute for Health and Aging, University of California, San Francisco; Injury Prevention Center, Johns Hopkins University, Baltimore, Md.

Scalea, T.M., H.M. Simon, A.O. Duncan, N.A. Atweh, J.A. Sclafani, T.F. Phillips, and G.W. Shaftan. 1990. Geriatric Blunt Multiple Trauma: Improved Survival with Early Invasive Monitoring. *Journal of Trauma,* Vol. 30, No. 2, pp. 129–136.

Schulz, J. 1989. Truckers' Hours of Service Rules to Receive Comprehensive

Study. *Traffic World*, Vol. 220, No. 10, Dec. 4, pp. 20–21.

Solomon, D. 1964. *Accidents on Main Rural Highways Related to Speed, Driver, and Vehicle.* Bureau of Public Roads, U. S. Department of Commerce, July.

Staplin, L., et al. 1987. *Age-Related Diminished Capabilities and Driver Performance.* Working Paper. FHWA, U.S. Department of Transportation.

TRB. 1987a. *Special Report 214: Designing Safer Roads: Practices for Resurfacing, Restoration, and Rehabilitation.* National Research Council, Washington, D.C., 319 pp.

TRB. 1987b. *Special Report 216: Zero Alcohol and Other Options: Limits for Truck and Bus Drivers.* National Research Council, Washington, D.C., 196 pp.

TRB. 1988. *Special Report 218: Transportation in an Aging Society: Improving Mobility and Safety for Older Persons,* Volume 1. National Research Council, Washington, D.C., 125 pp.

TRB. 1989a. *Special Report 223: Providing Access for Large Trucks.* National Research Council, Washington, D.C., 316 pp.

TRB. 1989b. *Special Report 224: Safety Belts, Airbags, and Child Restraints: Research To Address Emerging Policy Questions.* National Research Council, Washington, D.C., 69 pp.

TRB. 1989c. *Transportation Research Circular 349: Research Problem Statements: Operational Effects of Geometrics and Geometric Design.* National Research Council, Washington, D.C., April, 13 pp.

TRB. 1990. *Special Report 228: Data Requirements for Monitoring Truck Safety.* National Research Council, Washington, D.C.

U.S. Congress. House. 1989a. Committee on Appropriations. Department of Transportation and Related Agencies Appropriations for 1990. Hearings before 101st Congress, First Session, Part 4.

U.S. Congress. House. 1989b. Committee on Public Works and Transportation. *The Status of the Nation's Highways and Bridges: Conditions and Performance and Highway Bridge Replacement and Rehabilitation Program 1989.* Committee Print 101-2. Government Printing Office, Washington, D.C., June.

U.S. Congress. Senate. 1988. Committee on Commerce, Science and Transportation. *Motor Carrier Safety Assistance Program (MCSAP): Options Intended to Improve a Generally Successful and Cooperative Federal/State Partnership Promoting Truck and Bus Safety.* Committee Print 100-109. Government Printing Office, Washington, D.C.

U.S. Congress. Senate. 1989a. *Hearings before the Subcommittee on Surface Transportation of the Committee on Commerce, Science, and Transportation.* Report 101-145.

U.S. Congress. Senate. 1989b. Committee on Commerce, Science and Transportation. *Motor Carrier Safety and the Federal Highway Administration's Education and Enforcement Efforts: Options Intended to Improve an Overloaded Program.* Committee Print. Government Printing Office, Washington, D.C.

Viano, D.C. 1987. *Evaluation of the Benefit of Energy-Absorbing Material in Side-Impact Protection: Part II.* 872213. Society of Automotive Engineers, Warrendale, Pa.

Viano, D.C., I.V. Lau, C. Asbury, A. King, and P. Begeman. 1989a. Biomechanics of the Human Chest, Abdomen, and Pelvis in Lateral Impact. In *33rd Annual Proceedings, Association for the Advancement of Automotive Medicine.* AAAM, Arlington Heights, Ill., Oct.

Viano, D.C., I.V. Lau, D.V. Andrzejak, and C. Asbury. 1989b. Biomechanics of

Injury in Lateral Impacts. *Accident Prevention and Analysis,* Vol. 21, No. 6, Dec., pp. 535–551.

Viano, D.C., C.C. Culver, L. Evans, and M. Frick. 1990. Involvement of Older Drivers in Multi-Vehicle Side-Impact Crashes. *Accident Analysis and Prevention,* Vol. 22, No. 2, April, pp. 177–188.

Wallen, M. 1990. *Liability and the Setting of Agency Safety Priorities.* Institute of Transportation Engineers, March, 6 pp.

Waller, P.F. 1988. Renewal Licensing of Older Drivers. In *Special Report 218: Transportation in an Aging Society,* Volume 2, TRB, National Research Council, Washington, D.C., pp. 72–100.

4

Research To Address Persistent Highway Safety Problems

E ven if all of the research to address emerging highway safety problems suggested in Chapter 3 were conducted and implemented, major problems would remain. A well-structured highway safety research program should make adequate provision for continuing research on persistent safety problems as well.

ISSUES AND TOPICS FOR RESEARCH

Several of these persistent problems, the scale of the problem, and examples of where additional research could prove fruitful are given in Table 4-1.

Substance-Impaired Driving

Alcohol-impaired driving continues to be a major highway safety problem. In 1988 nearly 40 percent of all fatally injured drivers had blood alcohol concentrations (BACs) exceeding the legal limit, that is, BACs $\geq$ 0.10 percent[1] (NHTSA 1989, 2–5). Although this figure represents a 15 percent decline from 1982, the reasons for this decline are not fully understood (Evans et al. 1989).

The effect of other drugs on highway safety is less clear, but evidence of a problem is mounting. Recent surveys indicate a surprisingly high percentage of respondents admitting to driving after having consumed illicit drugs. In Vermont, for example, 16 percent of male respondents admitted to driving after using both alcohol and cocaine; the median use was 3.5 drinks and 3.5 lines of cocaine (Musty and Perrine 1989). In San

TABLE 4-1 RESEARCH AGENDA TO ADDRESS PERSISTENT HIGHWAY SAFETY PROBLEMS

Problem	Scale of Problem	Examples of Needed Research
Substance-impaired driving	Nearly 40 percent of fatally injured drivers legally intoxicated (i.e., BAC ≥ 0.10 percent)	Incidence of drug-impaired driving Effects of drugs on driver behavior Screening methods to detect drug-impaired driving Attitudes toward driving, alcohol, and drug use Alternative strategies to increase deterrence Effect of alcohol intoxication on injury survivability
Young drivers (under 25)	Vehicle occupant fatalities among 16- to 24-year-olds largest category of fatalities of any age group	Attitudes toward risk taking and driving Safety initiatives for the teenage driver
Pedestrians[a]	Nearly 7,000 pedestrians killed annually on the road away from intersections	Role of alcohol and drugs Pedestrian conspicuity Highway design and traffic control measures Vehicle design
Motorcyclists	Motorcycles nearly 14 times more likely to be involved in fatal crash than passenger vehicles; nearly 3,800 fatalities annually	Attitudes toward risk and injury reduction measures Motorcycle conspicuity
Bicyclists	Nearly 1,000 bicyclists killed annually on highways; growing share of traffic fatalities	Rider behavior and injury reduction measures Bicycle conspicuity Highway design measures
Driver inattention and error	Majority of vehicle occupant fatalities experienced by "average" driver (25 to 64)	The driving task Driver inattention and error in crash causation
Traffic law enforcement and adjudication	Effectiveness of traffic safety enforcement and adjudication process threatened by limited resources and overburdened courts	Opportunities for targeted enforcement Enforcement of bicycle and pedestrian laws Effectiveness of adjudication alternatives Public acceptance of enforcement and adjudication strategies

NOTE: BAC = blood alcohol concentration.
[a] Except older pedestrians, whose research needs are discussed in Chapter 3.

Bernardino County, complete drug screens have been administered to all fatally injured crash victims for the last 2.5 years; of the over 700 fatalities, 21 percent had illicit drugs in their bloodstream at the time of death (Root 1989). A study of 101 fatally injured drivers in Maryland found a similar incidence of illicit drugs (Caplan et al. 1989). Use of certain over-the-counter prescription drugs may also affect driving performance, particularly when they are mixed with alcohol.

The effect of alcohol consumption on traffic safety has long been recognized, and research on alcohol and safety, though not complete, is extensive. The same cannot be said for other drugs, particularly illicit drugs. Fundamental research is needed on the problems of driving under the influence of drugs other than alcohol. Additional research on alcohol and traffic safety is also indicated.

Incidence of Drug-Impaired Driving

The studies of drug abuse cited above, though fragmentary, show that drugs other than alcohol contribute to highway crashes. Compton's (1988) review of the literature suggests that 10 to 20 percent of crash-involved drivers have a drug other than alcohol in their bodies, often in combination with alcohol. Given the suggestive evidence just cited, more extensive studies to determine the size of the problem should be conducted. At present such research would be limited to more extensive blood tests of injured and killed crash victims and crash-involved drivers. In contrast to the alcohol safety area, where epidemiological studies can rely on breath tests to estimate the incidence of drinking and driving, simple screens for drug-impaired driving are not available.

Effects of Drugs on Driver Behavior

Hundreds of studies have examined the effects of alcohol on driving or skills related to driving (Moskowitz and Robinson 1988). Although many of these studies are flawed in some way, a consensus appears from a review of the best studies in this literature. The human response to alcohol, both physiologically and behaviorally, varies widely, but in general, driving-related skills are impaired as the amount of alcohol in the bloodstream rises; further, this effect is measurable after small doses of alcohol (equivalent to a single drink) (TRB 1987).

The effects of drugs other than alcohol (over-the-counter prescription drugs as well as illegal drugs) on performance is less well understood. In alcohol research, for example, intake can be compared on the basis of

BAC. With the BAC as a measure, the confounding effects of body size and metabolism can be controlled for as performance is studied. A similar measure for intake of most other drugs has proven elusive; this makes generalizations about the effect of varied levels of drug ingestion on behavior more difficult to make. In other words, research has not advanced far enough in this area to answer the basic question of whether, or how much, the presence of drugs in the bodies of fatally injured drivers or pedestrians contributed to the crash or to injury levels.

Research examining the behavioral effects of alcohol and other drugs has also suffered from crude experimental devices for measuring performance. Most laboratory studies can be criticized for lacking any real relationship to the driving task. Studies using simulators to better replicate driving have used simplistic devices. On-road studies using instrumented cars provide more realistic test conditions but are uncommon, particularly in the United States, because of concern for exposing subjects and others to risk; on-road studies examining high dose levels are out of the question. The U.S. Department of Transportation is currently cooperating with the West German government in research using the advanced simulator developed by Mercedes-Benz to study under more realistic driving situations impairing effects of drugs on driving-related behavior (Compton 1988).

Screening Methods To Detect Drug-Impaired Driving

A major impediment to estimating the incidence of drug use is the lack of good screening methods. Blood is currently the only body fluid that can indicate whether the subject might have been under the influence of the drug detected at the time the blood sample was collected, which is critical to determining whether the drug was linked to impaired driving performance (Compton 1988, 10). Research with blood samples, however, is both expensive and difficult; thus researchers have tended not to screen for a wide range of drugs (Compton 1988, 9). Recent advances in drug testing technology should provide researchers with a more accurate and precise determination of drug usage for a wider selection of drugs (Compton 1988, 36).

The expense and intrusiveness of current drug screening procedures has also limited on-the-road testing of drivers for drug use (Compton 1988, 33). However, methods to improve police detection of drug use by drivers are being developed and warrant further study. NHTSA has recently evaluated a drug recognition procedure developed by the Los Angeles Police Department that enables police officers to identify different types of drug impairment (Bigelow et al. 1985; Compton 1986). The procedure focuses on detecting the behavioral and physiological symptoms associated with the major categories of drugs (e.g., stimulants, depressants, and hallu-cinogens), enabling enforcement efforts and testing to be more highly targeted (Compton 1988, 38). Further development of such detection procedures could greatly enhance efforts to recognize and apprehend drug-impaired drivers.

Attitudes Toward Driving, Alcohol, and Drug Use

One explanation for the decline in alcohol-involved motor vehicle fatal-ities over the past decade is a fundamental change in social attitudes and behaviors about drinking and driving. However, few researchers have attempted to examine the role of changing social norms in alcohol-impaired driving behavior, in part because of the difficulty of separating the effects of broad changes in social norms from other factors that may influence alcohol use and driving. Some researchers maintain that the changes are only temporary; others suggest that deterrence is working because of highly visible enforcement strategies that raise the certainty of punishment for intoxicated drivers, such as checkpoints, preliminary breath tests, and license revocation laws; still others suggest a more fun-damental change in attitudes about alcohol use and driving that may be the root cause of the change (Howland 1988; Evans et al. 1989; Evans 1989). Understanding the interaction between laws and the development of new social norms (Howland 1988) and building on the considerable research that has been conducted on deterrence could help sort out the major factors responsible for recent trends in alcohol-impaired driving behavior and enable policy makers to take advantage of the current window of oppor-tunity to ensure that the desired changes become permanent. Social atti-tudes toward driving under the influence of drugs other than alcohol are largely unknown.

Alternative Strategies To Increase Deterrence

A growing body of literature has helped develop a better understanding of the appropriate levels of public information, enforcement, and legal sanc-tions required to deter the general population from undesired behavior, such as driving under the influence of alcohol. Enforcement strategies, such as crackdowns on alcohol-impaired driving through sobriety check-points and intensified patrols, have successfully reduced the incidence of alcohol-impaired driving in the short term (Voas 1988). However, more needs to be known about the most efficient strategies and the frequency with which they must be repeated in order to sustain or increase their effects. The necessary components of public information programs also must be refined. The type of message, amount and type of media exposure, and the most efficient means of communication remain to be determined by research.

Sanctions affect deterrence by increasing the perception that those apprehended will be punished. Although popular sentiment appears to support tougher criminal sanctions for alcohol-impaired driving, evaluations of such policies in the United States show that they have no effect (Ross 1989). Nichols and Ross (1989), after reviewing the literature evaluating the effect of different sanctions, suggest that stiffer fines and license withdrawals are more likely to have a general deterrent effect than other legal penalties, and further believe that by handling these cases administratively, the punishment can be meted out more quickly. More extensive evaluative research is needed to confirm these hypotheses, to define how swift the process must be and the appropriate level of fines or driving restrictions, and to define more clearly the supportive role of education for offenders and public information campaigns to remind the general public of the threat.

Interventions that are effective in deterring the general population from alcohol-impaired driving may not have the same deterrent effect on those who are already intoxicated. More needs to be known about measures that will affect the behavior of potential drivers who already have an elevated BAC.

Effect of Alcohol Intoxication on Injury Survivability

Researchers have found that drivers with BACs exceeding the legal limit (i.e., BACs ≥ 0.10 percent) at the time of a motor vehicle crash are more likely to suffer serious injury or death, taking into account other crash variables that contribute to driver injury, compared with nondrinking drivers (Waller et al. 1986, Stewart 1989). Alcohol complicates the ability of the body to recover from trauma. Laboratory studies using animals have confirmed the adverse physiological effects of high levels of alcohol on injury severity, particularly on cardiac and spinal cord injuries that are experienced in motor vehicle crashes (Anderson and Viano 1986, 3). Better understanding of the nature and extent of the effects of acute alcohol use on motor vehicle injury, including long- as well as short-term effects, should improve treatment strategies for crash-involved drivers at elevated BACs.

Young Drivers

The aging of the population should result in some decline in traffic deaths among the young, but drivers and other vehicle occupants under age 25 are still likely to constitute the single largest category of all occupant fatalities for the foreseeable future (Figure 1-6).

Young drivers typically have the best visual ability and reaction times of drivers of all age groups, but often display poor judgment. Young men, in particular, are much more likely than other drivers to drive while impaired by alcohol or other drugs, to speed, to fail to wear safety belts, and to be involved in higher-speed, single-vehicle crashes (Peck 1985; Jonah 1986; TRB 1989). Young women are beginning to exhibit similar behaviors (*Highway Safety Directions* 1990). Continuing research is needed in at least two broad areas on ways to reduce crash risk for young drivers.

Attitudes Toward Risk Taking and Driving

Young drivers often tend to engage in risk-taking behaviors, such as speeding and not wearing safety belts, which, combined with their more limited driving experience, result in higher crash rates. Recent research (Beirness and Simpson 1988, 203) suggests that risky driving among youth is part of a more general adolescent lifestyle that encompasses a number of other adolescent problem behaviors, such as drug use and heavy drinking, that are manifested outside of the driving situation as well. Better understanding of the factors that encourage risk-taking behaviors could help identify ways of reaching youthful drivers that could complement, and potentially enhance, traditional educational or law enforcement approaches. For example, a recent study of safety belt use among high school students in Maryland found that belt use increased among teenage drivers after the state passed a mandatory safety belt use law, but was still lower (by 6 to 38 percentage points) than among comparison drivers from the surrounding community (Wells et al. 1989, 3). The study recommended measures such as making school parking privileges contingent on wearing safety belts combined with more intensive enforcement as more likely to influence behavior than techniques based solely on persuasion (Wells et al. 1989, 4). The efficacy of combining education and enforcement with incentive programs merits further study.

Safety Initiatives for the Teenage Driver

Another profitable area for research is on ways to improve entry driver programs and licensing practices for teenage drivers. The effectiveness of traditional driver education programs has been challenged. A major study of the value of driver education in secondary schools (Stock et al. 1983) found no statistically significant differences in the number of crashes and violations between teenage students who had received training and a control group who had not.[2] However, because the students that had received driver education were licensed sooner than the control group, it could be said that the former were able to drive earlier without a significant increase in crashes and violations. Other studies (Lund et al. 1986; Robertson 1980) found that the availability of high school driver education programs causes students to become licensed earlier, increasing their exposure at an earlier age. Provisional or graduated licensing programs that spread training over a longer period, gradually increasing exposure to more difficult driving situations, and make licensing privileges directly dependent on safe performance provide an alternative approach to many current state programs.[3] Although two-thirds of the states impose some form of restriction on young drivers, only a few states like California and Maryland have adopted a comprehensive new driver entry system (Tannahill and Smith 1990, 20). More research is needed on the effectiveness of these alternative approaches and the potential barriers to their acceptance by other states.

Pedestrians

Motor vehicles strike and kill nearly 7,000 pedestrians each year (NHTSA 1989, 8-7). Although pedestrian fatalities declined at roughly twice the rate of total fatalities over the past decade, pedestrian deaths from motor vehicle crashes still represent about 15 percent of total annual motor vehicle fatalities (NHTSA 1989, 8-7). Pedestrian and other nonoccupant fatalities are likely to increase as the population ages (Figure 1-7).

Although considerable research on pedestrian issues was conducted during the 1970s, public funding for this purpose was sharply reduced during the 1980s (Table A-1). Renewed research in at least four areas could prove fruitful. (Research needs for the older pedestrian are discussed in Chapter 3.)

Role of Alcohol and Drugs

Alcohol is a major factor contributing to pedestrian fatalities. In 1988 nearly one-third of all pedestrians (and bicyclists) involved in fatal motor vehicle crashes were at BAC levels that would have made it illegal for them to drive (BACs ≥ 0.10 percent); in comparison, nearly one-fourth of all drivers involved in fatal crashes were legally intoxicated (NHTSA 1989, 2-4, 2-11). The share of intoxicated pedestrians in fatal crashes is highest for those between the ages of 20 and 64, and has remained relatively stable over the past decade (NHTSA 1989, 2-11), suggesting that drunk driving countermeasures may not be reaching adult pedestrians. However, little is known about this population and even less about the role of drug use, either alone or in combination with alcohol, in pedestrian involvements in fatal crashes. Better understanding of the nature of the problem could lead to more appropriate solutions than have yet been devised.

Pedestrian Conspicuity

More than twice as many pedestrian fatalities occur at night as during daylight hours (NHTSA 1989, 8-11). Making pedestrians more visible to drivers could reduce crash risk. Many measures to enhance visibility of pedestrians, such as flashlights and retroreflective clothing, are available, but they are not widely used. More attention should be given to identifying ways of promoting conspicuity, from involving the fashion industry to publicity campaigns to targeting and motivating likely pedestrian users (TRB 1988c, 11). The costs and effectiveness of alternative measures should also be evaluated.

Highway Design and Traffic Control Measures

The safety benefits of many design and operational measures to reduce the risk of pedestrian crashes are not well established. For example, about one-fifth of all pedestrian fatalities occur at intersections and over half of these intersections are not controlled by signs or signals (Hauer 1988, 199, 200). However, the safety effects, on both pedestrians and drivers, of installing traffic signals, stop signs, or yield signs at intersections are poorly understood (Hauer 1988, 247). Similarly, there is conflicting evidence on the safety benefits of another common measure to enhance pedestrian safety, marked crosswalks (Hauer 1988, 245). Little or no follow-up research has been done to determine whether current specifications for channeling pedestrians through urban work zones are enhancing pedestrian safety (TRB 1988c, 4). More needs to be known about the costs and benefits of these pedestrian-related highway design and operating measures, so that they can be given more adequate consideration, particularly when such a high priority is being placed on measures to improve highway capacity and traffic flow. More study of appropriate treatments for nonintersection crash sites, where the majority of pedestrian fatalities occur, could also prove beneficial.

Vehicle Design

The design of several vehicle features, including bumpers and hoods, can affect the severity of injury when a pedestrian comes into contact with a motor vehicle. Measures to afford pedestrians greater protection, such as softer and more uniform vehicle fronts in the area where the pedestrian's head is likely to strike the vehicle during impact, and lower bumpers to reduce the probability of pelvic and leg fractures, have been proposed (TRB 1988a, 89; IIHS 1989, 15). Determining optimal solutions, however, is not easy. Pedestrians range in size from small children to adults, and this range affects the choice of optimal bumper height. Vehicle design changes such as bumper height can affect the height of other safety hardware, such as roadside barriers. Pedestrians differ across age groups in their tolerance to different kinds of injuries resulting from pedestrian-car crashes, differences which also affect the choice of optimal external vehicle design. And finally, the costs of design changes must be weighed against the expected level of safety gains. All of these topics merit more research if the potential for design improvements to enhance pedestrian safety is to be realized.

Motorcyclists

Fatalities among motorcycle riders represent a sizeable share of all traffic deaths each year. Although fatal motorcycle crashes have declined since the mid-1980s, fatalities in motorcycle crashes reached nearly 3,800 in 1988 or about 8 percent of all traffic fatalities (NHTSA 1989, 6-18, 6-20). Per mile traveled, a motorcycle is about 14 times more likely than a passenger car to be involved in a fatal crash (NHTSA 1989, 6-5; FHWA 1989, 172), and in the majority of crashes, it is the motorcycle driver who is killed (NHTSA 1989, 6–20). Crash data indicate that head trauma accounts for 70 percent of deaths among motorcycle riders (statement of Jerry Ralph Curry, NHTSA Administrator, before the Transportation Subcommittee of the Committee on Appropriations, U.S. Senate, April 5, 1990).

Attitudes Toward Risk and Injury Reduction Measures

Motorcyclists as a group exhibit many risk-taking behaviors, including drinking and driving and not wearing helmets. In 1988, for example, more than one-third of motorcycle drivers involved in a fatal crash were intoxicated, the highest of any vehicle group (NHTSA 1989, 2-8). Helmets have proven to be 29 percent effective in reducing motorcycle driver and passenger fatalities in a crash (Wilson 1989, 1), but helmet use is far from universal; only 23 states require riders to wear helmets (statement of Jerry Ralph Curry, NHTSA Administrator, before the Transportation Subcommittee of the Committee on Appropriations, U.S. Senate, April 5, 1990). Many methods of reducing crash risk among motorcycle drivers have been identified, such as motorcycle operator training programs, more stringent licensing and testing procedures, and alcohol deterrence measures like license suspension, but further evaluation is needed. Helmet use laws appear to have a good potential for reducing injuries sustained in motorcycle crashes, because compliance with these laws appears to be high (statement of Jerry Ralph Curry, NHTSA Administrator, before the Transportation Subcommittee of the Committee on Appropriations, U.S. Senate, April 5, 1990).

Motorcycle Conspicuity

One of the factors that may contribute to motorcycle crashes is the motorcycle's small profile, which makes it very difficult to detect in a head-on position (TRB 1986, 3). Measures to increase motorcycle and driver conspicuity, such as daytime use of headlights and fluorescent garments, and nighttime use of running lights and retroreflective clothing, have been suggested; some of the measures have been tested in the field (Olson et al. 1979). However, their effectiveness in reducing crash risk and their impact on other motorists (glare, distraction, etc.) warrant further study before these measures are likely to be accepted or adopted.

Bicyclists

Bicyclist fatalities represent a relatively small (approximately 2 percent) but persistent share of highway fatalities. In 1988 there were 910 such fatalities; 30 percent of those killed were children aged 10 to 17 (NHTSA 1989, 8-13). The number of bicycle fatalities is likely to increase if bicycle sales continue to grow as they have over the past decade, raising the exposure of this vulnerable group. To date, research on measures to improve bicycle safety has been limited.

Rider Behavior and Injury Reduction Measures

An in-depth study of fatal bicycle–motor vehicle crashes found that the majority were the result of inattention, inappropriate behavior, and error on the part of the bicycle rider and the driver of the motor vehicle (Cross and Fisher 1977, 19). Although follow-up research on appropriate countermeasures was conducted (Blomberg et al. 1982), little funding has been available to implement the findings and evaluate promising strategies. Further understanding of bicyclist safety is likely to require revisiting prior research to identify which riding behaviors have the greatest potential for preventing conflict with a motor vehicle, studying the range of knowledge and skills among different types of operators (TRB 1988b), and determining the extent to which bicyclists (and motor vehicle operators) observe current traffic laws. In the absence of any licensing process for bicycles, this information would be helpful in developing education programs targeted at specific bicycle users (children, bicycle commuters, etc.) as well as operators of motor vehicles.

Helmet use is known to be effective in reducing head injuries, which are a leading cause of death in bicycle crashes. A recent study found that helmet use by bicyclists can cut the risk of a head injury by 85 percent and brain injury by 88 percent (Thompson et al. 1989, 1,365). Yet many bicyclists, particularly children, do not wear helmets (Thompson et al. 1989, 1,366). The research tasks are to identify the extent of helmet use, reasons for use and nonuse, and effective strategies and incentives for increasing use.

Bicycle Conspicuity

More than 40 percent of fatal traffic crashes involving bicycles take place between dusk and dawn (NHTSA 1989, 8-12). Research has identified several options for improving the lighting and reflectivity of bicycles and bicyclists, particularly in poor light conditions (Hale and Zeidler 1984; Blomberg et al. 1986). Some improvements have been implemented. For example, the Consumer Product Safety Commission requires that all bicycles come equipped with reflectors in the wheels and on the pedals. However, more work is needed to identify the relative efficacy and cost of the most promising options as well as ways of motivating the sports industry to promote, and bicyclists to use, these countermeasures. Because many of the measures for improving bicyclist conspicuity are also appropriate for pedestrians, opportunities for joint research are promising.

Highway Design Measures

If bicyclists are to share the highways with motor vehicle traffic, highway designers should pay more attention to identifying and minimizing roadway hazards for cyclists (TRB 1988b, 8). For example, speed bumps may reduce motor vehicle traffic speed in a residential neighborhood but may present hazardous obstacles for cyclists.

One alternative for reducing conflict potential is simply to separate bicycle traffic through dedicated bike lanes or separate bicycle paths. However, some of these proposals appear to be at odds with measures to reduce congestion, such as using shoulders as vehicle lanes during peak traffic periods. A more comprehensive review of alternative strategies and their relative costs and benefits could help identify and resolve potential areas of conflict.

Driver Inattention and Error

Although the rates of driver involvement in crashes are higher for certain age groups, such as the young and the old, the total number of involvements is greatest for those drivers between the ages of 25 and 64 (Figure 1-5). From a skills perspective, this group of drivers, on average, presumably has the best combination of experience, judgment, and physical capabilities of any age group. Yet driver inattention and failure to see have been identified as major contributing factors to motor vehicle crashes for drivers of all ages (Malliaris et al. 1983).

New electronics and communications technologies are being developed with the potential for reducing the risk of collisions by providing drivers with additional information and possibly automating certain functions. The importance of an expanded program of human factors research to the success of these efforts has been noted. However, there are still considerable gaps in knowledge about crash causation and the interaction between drivers and vehicles equipped with today's technology that must be addressed if advances are to be made in crash avoidance.

The Driving Task

Driving requires the performance of perceptual, cognitive, and physical tasks (TRB 1988a). In-depth studies of the skills involved in driving have not been conducted since the 1960s when human factors researchers examined driver perception-reaction behavior, such as lane tracking, sign reading, and object avoidance on high-speed roads (FHWA 1976, 349). These studies should be updated in light of today's driving population, vehicles, and highway conditions. Specific attention should be paid to defining and measuring driver workload, including the factors that influence workload and their effect on driving performance; defining driver visual capacity and search patterns, particularly nighttime visibility requirements and the effect of glare on nighttime perception; and driver decision-making and vehicle control skills (i.e., perception-decision-response times). Some research along these lines has been conducted for the older driver, which should be extended to the general driving population.

Driver Inattention and Error in Causing Crashes

Many motor vehicle crashes occur from common causes, such as inattention or fatigue-induced errors. However, crash data provide little information on the behavioral antecedents of crashes, making analysis difficult. Developing a taxonomy of the different types of driver errors of commission and omission that contribute to motor vehicle crashes would provide a logical starting point for a more in-depth analysis of their role in crash causation. Considerable attention has recently been given to the role of fatigue in motor vehicle crashes (Moskowitz 1989). Although much of the research has focused on the commercial driver, defining and measuring driver fatigue and its effect on driving performance should have broad application for devising countermeasures to reduce fatigue-induced errors in the general driving population. Better understanding of the attentional capacities of drivers, particularly in complex traffic situations, and driver reaction-response capabilities in emergency situations could help pinpoint opportunities for improved driver training and new technological aids for the driver.

Traffic Law Enforcement and Adjudication

Traffic law enforcement and adjudication have an important role to play in addressing many of the persistent safety problems raised in this chapter. The success of many traffic safety countermeasures—safety belt use laws, sobriety checkpoints, and maximum speed limits—depends on large-scale behavioral changes, which in turn depend partly on the effectiveness of the police and the courts in detecting, apprehending, and sanctioning violators.

Law enforcement agency managers, however, often have difficulty justifying the resources they require for adequate enforcement. While most communities suffer greater losses from motor vehicle crashes than from criminal activity (Streff and Molnar 1990), there is usually more citizen pressure to "do something" about crime than about traffic safety. Moreover, the courts are overburdened with cases that may take priority over traffic violations. Law enforcement agency managers need assistance in both convincing others of the need for traffic enforcement and making the most out of the resources they are given.

Opportunities for improving the efficiency of enforcement through automated technologies and the research needed to realize these opportunities were discussed in Chapter 3. The research topics suggested here focus on nontechnological approaches to improving the efficacy of the enforcement and adjudication process.

Opportunities for Targeted Enforcement

Targeted enforcement strategies to deter alcohol-impaired driving and encourage safety belt use have shown positive results (Voas 1988; Williams and Lund 1988). For example, highly visible enforcement coupled with extensive public information increased safety belt use in a test city from 49 to 77 percent, whereas a comparison city showed no change. Belt use declined when measured 4 months after the program ended, but was still 66 percent, which was higher than before (Williams et al. 1987). Successful but short-term benefits have also been obtained in crackdowns on alcohol-impaired driving through sobriety checkpoints and intensified patrols (Voas 1988). The cost and capability of extending these benefits for a longer time and generalizing them to a broader population, however, have not been determined. Nor has the appropriate mix of public information, enforcement, incentives, and sanctions been adequately studied.

Innovative Approaches to Enforcement of Bicycle and Pedestrian Laws

In many law enforcement agencies, enforcement of bicycle and pedestrian laws is a low priority or totally ignored. This situation often stems from a lack of awareness by the police of the seriousness of the problem. Understanding why bicyclists and pedestrians violate traffic laws, how they perceive risk, and what factors motivate safe behavior should help in the design of appropriate enforcement strategies and public information campaigns to address the problem. Part of the research should focus on ways to sensitize the police to the magnitude of the problem and develop their support for greater involvement in its resolution. A particularly difficult issue is the problem of intoxicated pedestrians, because many states have decriminalized public intoxication. Research can help devise policies that will insure that the police can take legal action against intoxicated pedestrians who pose a traffic safety threat.

Effectiveness of Adjudication Alternatives

The effectiveness of many traffic safety countermeasures depends also on sanctions for violators. However, the court system is often unable to handle some traffic law violations expeditiously. Alternatives to criminal sanctions, such as fines and license revocation, have been shown to be effective in deterring alcohol-impaired driving (Nichols and Ross 1989); administrative adjudication of these cases has also increased the swiftness and certainty of punishment. Opportunities for nonjudicial resolution of other traffic violations should be explored as well as opportunities for positive incentives to encourage compliance with traffic laws.

Public Acceptance of Enforcement and Adjudication Strategies

Drivers routinely disregard traffic laws by driving in excess of the speed limit, tailgating, running red lights, and driving intoxicated, and some would argue that these behaviors are on the increase (Deacon 1988, 20). Research is needed to understand better the reasons for disregard of traffic laws. Is it a by-product of the stress created by congestion that encourages drivers to ignore traffic control devices, disobey rules of the road, and even engage in violent behavior (Deacon 1988, 20)? Is it part of a broader social phenomenon of growing disregard for authority that is manifested in other behavioral patterns, such as increased illicit drug use? Is it the laws themselves that appear unreasonable and outdated to drivers, given the capabilities of today's vehicles and improved highway conditions? Or is it that the laws stand in the way of what people want to do? Answering these questions and understanding the factors that motivate unsafe behavior are important to modifying behavior, to knowing what enforcement strategies are likely to prove most effective, and what level of enforcement is appropriate and likely to be tolerated by society.

SUMMARY

Many promising areas for research have been identified that may enable further advances in tackling difficult and persistent highway safety problems. New advances are likely, however, only if the research is organized and managed in a way that will encourage innovative and sound research approaches, an issue that is discussed in Chapter 5.

NOTES

1. Blood alcohol concentration is the standard measure of intoxication. A BAC of 0.10 percent means a level of 0.10 g of pure alcohol per 100 ml of blood.

2. Preliminary results from a follow-up evaluation of the DeKalb study, which tracked the control and experimental groups through 6 years of driving experience, indicated a significant difference in the number of crashes and violations between those students who had received some minimum training and the control group (Smith 1987, 4). However, there were no significant differences in the number of crashes between those students who had received extensive training and the control group.
3. The comprehensive driver entry system advocated by NHTSA and the American Association of Motor Vehicle Administrators includes the following features: (*a*) learner's permit; (*b*) parent-supervised driving practice, including nighttime driving; (*c*) nighttime restriction except for supervised driving; (*d*) legal drinking age of 21 and zero blood alcohol concentration for under-age drivers; (*e*) mandatory safety belt usage by all vehicle occupants; (*f*) no crashes or convictions within a specified time; (*g*) prompt restrictions after crashes or convictions; and (*h*) a distinct provisional license (Tannahill and Smith 1990, 19).

REFERENCES

ABBREVIATIONS

FHWA	Federal Highway Administration
IIHS	Insurance Institute for Highway Safety
NHTSA	National Highway Traffic Safety Administration
TRB	Transportation Research Board

Anderson, T.E., and D.C. Viano. 1986. *Effect of Acute Alcohol Intoxication on Injury Tolerance and Outcome.* GMR-5548. General Motors Research Laboratories, Warren, Mich. Sept. 9.

Beirness, D.J., and H.M. Simpson. 1988. Lifestyle Correlates of Risky Driving and Accident Involvement Among Youth. *Alcohol, Drugs and Driving,* Vol. 4, No. 3–4, July–Dec., pp. 193–204.

Bigelow, G.E., W.E. Bickel, J.D. Roache, I.A. Liebson, and P. Nowowieski. 1985. *Identifying Types of Drug Intoxication: Laboratory Evaluation of a Subject-Examination Procedure.* NHTSA, U.S. Department of Transportation, May, 44 pp.

Blomberg, R.D., W.A. Leaf, A. Hale, M.L. Farrell, and K.D. Cross. 1982. *Identification and Development of Countermeasures for Bicyclist/Motor Vehicle Problem Types.* Report DOT HS-7-01726, NHTSA, U.S. Department of Transportation, Aug.

Blomberg, R.D., A. Hale, and D.F. Preusser. 1986. Experimental Evaluation of Alternative Conspicuity Enhancement Techniques for Pedestrians and Bicyclists. *Journal of Safety Research,* Vol. 17, No. 1, pp. 1–12.

Caplan, Y., B. Levine, and B. Goldberger. 1989. *Drugs in Driver Fatalities: A Preliminary Study in the State of Maryland.* Presented at the 11th International Conference on Alcohol, Drugs, and Traffic Safety, Chicago, Ill., Oct.

Compton, R. 1986. *Field Evaluation of the Los Angeles Police Department Drug Detection Procedure.* Report DOT-HS-807-012. NHTSA, U.S. Department of Transportation, Feb.

Compton, R. 1988. *Use of Controlled Substances and Highway Safety: A Report to Congress.* Report DOT-HS-807-261. NHTSA, U.S. Department of Transportation, March, 44 pp.

Cross, K.D., and G. Fisher. 1977. *A Study of Bicycle/Motor-Vehicle Accidents: Identification of Problem Types and Countermeasure Approaches,* Volume 1. Report DOT-HS-803-315. NHTSA, U.S. Department of Transportation, Sept., 304 pp.

Deacon, J.A. 1988. *Highway Safety Research, Development, and Technology Transfer.* Research Report KTC-88-1. Kentucky Transportation Center, University of Kentucky, Lexington, Aug. 30, 27 pp.

Evans, L. 1989. *An Attempt to Categorize the Main Determinants of Traffic Safety.* GMR-6645. General Motors Research Laboratories, Warren, Mich., April 5, 26 pp.

Evans, W.N., D. Neville, and J.D. Graham. 1989. *General Deterrence of Drunk Driving: Evaluation of Recent American Policies.* Centers for Disease Control, New England Injury Prevention Research Center, and Canadian Health Research and Development Program, May 1, 37 pp.

FHWA. 1976. *America's Highways: 1776–1976.* U.S. Department of Transportation.

FHWA. 1989. *Highway Statistics 1988.* U.S. Department of Transportation.

Hale, A., and P. Zeidler. 1984. *Review of the Literature and Programs for Pedestrian and Bicyclist Conspicuity.* Report DOT-HS-806-564. NHTSA, U.S. Department of Transportation, April, 76 pp.

Hauer, E. 1988. The Safety of Older Persons at Intersections. In *Special Report 218: Transportation in an Aging Society,* Volume 2, TRB, National Research Council, Washington, D.C., pp. 194–252.

Highway Safety Directions. 1990. Young Women and Alcohol. Vol. 2, No. 3, Winter, pp. 4–6.

Howland, J. 1988. Social Norms and Drunk Driving Countermeasures. In *Preventing Automobile Injury* (J.D. Graham, ed.), Auburn House Publishing Company, Dover, Mass.

IIHS. 1989. *Twenty Years of Accomplishments by the Insurance Institute for Highway Safety.* Arlington, Va., 46 pp.

Jonah, B. (ed.). 1986. *Accident Analysis and Prevention,* Vol. 18, No. 4 (Special Issue: Youth and Traffic Accident Risk).

Lund, A.K., A.F. Williams, and P. Zador. 1986. High School Driver Education: Further Evaluation of the DeKalb County Study. *Accident Analysis and Prevention,* Vol. 18, No. 4, pp. 349–357.

Malliaris, A., R. Nicholson, J. Hedlund, and S. Schneider. 1983. *Crash Avoidance Research.* SAE SP-544. Society of Automotive Engineers, Warrendale, Pa.

Moskowitz, H. (ed.). 1989. Fatigue, Sleep Deprivation, Circadian Rhythms and Their Interaction with Alcohol and Other Drugs (Proceedings of an International Symposium). *Alcohol, Drugs and Driving,* Vol. 5, No. 3.

Moskowitz, H., and C. Robinson. 1988. *Effects of Low Doses of Alcohol on Driving-Related Skills: A Review of the Evidence.* Report DOT HS-807-280. NHTSA, U.S. Department of Transportation.

Musty, R., and M.W. Perrine. 1989. *Use of Drugs and Alcohol During Driving in Vermont.* Presented at the 11th International Conference on Alcohol, Drugs, and Traffic Safety, Chicago, Ill., Oct.

NHTSA. 1989. *Fatal Accident Reporting System 1988.* Report DOT HS-807-507. U.S. Department of Transportation, Dec.

Nichols, J., and H. Ross. 1989. The Effectiveness of Legal Sanctions in Dealing with Drinking Drivers. In *Background Papers, Surgeon General's Workshop on Drunk Driving,* U.S. Department of Health and Human Services.

Olson, P.L., R. Halstead-Nusslock, and M. Sivak. 1979. *Development and Testing of Techniques for Increasing the Conspicuity of Motorcycles and Motorcycle Drivers.* Report DOT-HS-805-143. NHTSA, U.S. Department of Transportation, October, 149 pp.

Peck, R. 1985. The Role of Youth in Traffic Accidents: A Review of Past and Current California Data. *Alcohol, Drugs, and Driving,* Vol. 1, No. 1–2, Jan–June.

Robertson, L.S. 1980. Crash Involvement of Teenaged Drivers When Driver Education is Eliminated from High School. *American Journal of Public Health,* Vol. 70, No. 6, June, pp. 599–603.

Root, I. 1989. *Illicit Drugs of Abuse in Traffic Fatalities.* Presented at the 11th International Conference on Alcohol, Drugs, and Traffic Safety, Chicago, Ill., Oct.

Ross, H. 1989. *The New Philadelphia Story: The Effects of Severe Penalties on Drunk Driving.* AAA Foundation for Traffic Safety, Washington, D.C.

Smith, M.F. 1987. *Summary of Preliminary Results: Follow-Up Evaluation Safe Performance Curriculum Driver Education Project.* Presented at the Annual Conference of the American Driver and Traffic Safety Education Association, Spokane, Wash., Aug. 10.

Stewart, J.R. 1989. Estimating the Effects Over Time of Alcohol on Injury Severity. *Accident Analysis and Prevention,* Vol. 21, No. 6, Dec., pp. 575–579.

Stock, J.R., J.K. Weaver, H.W. Ray, J.R. Brink, and M.G. Sadof. 1983. *Evaluation of Safe Performance Secondary School Driver Education Curriculum Demonstration Project.* Report DOT HS-806-568. Battelle Columbus Laboratories, Columbus, Ohio, June.

Streff, F.M. and L.J. Molnar. 1990. *Estimating Costs of Traffic Crashes and Index Crimes: Tools for Improved Decision Making.* The University of Michigan Transportation Research Institute, Ann Arbor, Michigan, July.

Tannahill, J., and M. Smith. 1990. States' Experience with Inexperienced Drivers. *Traffic Safety,* Vol. 90, No. 1, Jan./Feb., pp. 18–21.

Thompson, R.S., F.P. Rivara, and D.C. Thompson. 1989. A Case-Control Study of the Effectiveness of Bicycle Safety Helmets. *New England Journal of Medicine,* Vol. 320, No. 21, May, pp. 1361–1367.

TRB. 1986. *Transportation Research Circular 302: Motorcycle Design: Observations on Status and Research Needs.* National Research Council, Washington, D.C., April, 4 pp.

TRB. 1987. *Special Report 216: Zero Alcohol and Other Options: Limits for Truck and Bus Drivers.* National Research Council, Washington, D.C.

TRB. 1988a. *Special Report 218: Transportation in an Aging Society: Improving Mobility and Safety for Older Persons,* 2 volumes. National Research Council, Washington, D.C.

TRB. 1988b. *Transportation Research Circular 337: Bicycling and Bicycle Facilities Research Problem Statements.* National Research Council, Washington, D.C., Oct. 26 pp.

TRB. 1988c. *Transportation Research Circular 339: Research Problem Statements: Pedestrians.* National Research Council, Washington, D.C., Nov., 22 pp.

TRB. 1989. *Special Report 224: Safety Belts, Airbags, and Child Restraints: Research To Address Emerging Policy Questions.* National Research Council, Washington, D.C., 69 pp.

Voas, R. 1988. Comments on Paper by J. Howland, Social Norms and Drunk Driving Countermeasures. In *Preventing Automobile Injury: New Findings from Evaluation Research* (J. Graham, ed.), Auburn House, Dover, Mass., pp. 188–196.

Waller, P.F., J.R. Stewart, A.R. Hansen, J.C. Stutts, C.L. Popkin, and E.A. Rodgman. 1986. The Potentiating Effects of Alcohol on Driver Injury. *Journal of the American Medical Association,* Vol. 256, No. 11, Sept. 19, pp. 1461–1466.

Wells, J.K., A.F. Williams, N.J. Teed, and A.K. Lund. 1989. *Belt Use Among High School Students.* Insurance Institute for Highway Safety, Arlington, Va., Jan., 5 pp.

Williams, A., and A. Lund. 1988. Mandatory Seat Belt Use Laws and Occupant Crash Protection in the United States: Present Status and Future Prospects. In *Preventing Automobile Injury: New Findings from Evaluation Research* (J. Graham, ed.), Auburn House, Dover, Mass., pp. 51–72.

Williams, A., D. Preusser, R. Blomberg, and A. Lund. 1987. Seat Belt Use Law Enforcement and Publicity in Elmira, NY: A Reminder Campaign. *American Journal of Public Health,* Vol. 77, No. 11, pp. 1450–1451.

Wilson, D.C. 1989. *The Effectiveness of Motorcycle Helmets in Preventing Fatalities.* Report DOT-HS-807-416. NHTSA, U.S. Department of Transportation, March, 8 pp.

5

Improving the Management of Highway Safety Research

I nnovative, forward-looking research is needed to respond to current and emerging highway safety problems. However, there are limitations in the structure of existing highway safety research programs and the methods of conducting research. Institutional changes to help create an environment more conducive to innovation and scholarship are recommended.

LIMITATIONS OF CURRENT PROGRAMS

Shortcomings in the way that research on highway safety is currently organized and managed limit the effective use of resources and thus the contribution that research can make to solving highway safety problems.

Limited Continuity

Federal funding for highway safety research, which is vital to generating new ideas, has been cut over the past decade. The major casualty of the cutbacks was the funding of long-term research programs at the National Highway Traffic Safety Administration (NHTSA) and the Federal Highway Administration (FHWA). Because research budgets were cut, some program areas were eliminated and the scope of others was narrowed as the agencies emphasized short-term research in support of regulatory and programmatic activities. In recent years, sustained funding has been unavailable to support multiyear research programs of any size in key areas such as human factors and biomechanics. Without this funding to advance the knowledge base, the agencies are often in a reactive posture, poorly positioned to take the lead in addressing emerging safety problems.

As federal funding has been cut back, the capacity to sustain research expertise in relevant research disciplines has also dwindled. For example, there are few graduate programs in biomechanics, and many human factors specialists who were working on highway safety issues have switched to aviation issues, where funding is more abundant.[1] Those with new doctoral degrees are reluctant to build a career in these and other research areas where funding is limited and uncertain.

The short-term focus of many federal highway safety research programs has frequently been exacerbated by the changing political priorities of top administrators and an emphasis on projects that can produce results quickly.

Untested Scientific Merit

Awarding research funds through an investigator-initiated competitive process that subjects the merits of proposals to external peer review assures participation by members of the scientific community in evaluating both the relevance and methodological soundness of the proposed research. The majority of federal highway safety research funds are provided by the U.S. Department of Transportation (DOT) through a contracting process that relies on agency evaluation only; technical soundness of the research proposals is not subjected to the rigors of outside peer review. Moreover, little of the research appears in refereed publications. As a result, the scientific integrity of much of the research is not fully evaluated, and the broader academic community may not always be aware of the research that has been conducted. An exception is the Injury Control Program of the Centers for Disease Control (CDC), which provides research grants through a peer review process external to the agency.

Lack of Perceived Independence

The highway safety research field has not adequately developed the science base for vehicle regulation. As a result, the process of regulating automobile safety has often been adversarial, pitting the private against the public sector (Graham 1989, 234–235). A good example of problems created by the lack of an independent research perspective is the current controversy between government and industry over NHTSA's proposed side-impact standard. The level of funding required to conduct scientific studies and testing to evaluate the technical merits of industry's or government's position has not been forthcoming, making adjudication of their differences difficult.

Many of the shortcomings in the way that highway research funds are managed have been raised before. At the Dulles Conference, conducted by the Transportation Research Board in 1979 on NHTSA's Highway Safety Research, Development, and Demonstration Program, the absence of long-range, fundamental research to establish the knowledge base for development of specific countermeasures and regulations was criticized (TRB 1979, 39–40).

Today perhaps more than in 1979, the situation is conducive to addressing these concerns. Safety is a top priority of the current DOT administration (DOT 1990, 7), and research is recognized as a crucial component to addressing the growing and changing demands on the transportation system. DOT views its role as stimulating research initiatives by "creating an overall climate for new ideas and new approaches for transportation" (DOT 1990, 35).

MECHANISMS FOR FUNDING

As an introduction to the discussion of desired changes in the way that highway safety research is currently managed, an overview is provided here of the basic mechanisms used to fund research and their application in the highway safety research field.

There are two basic ways of funding research. First, funds may be provided to in-house agency staff to conduct their own research; this is known as intramural funding. Second, funds may be provided to external organizations or individuals who conduct the research; these extramural funds are generally distributed by contracts, grants, or cooperative agreements. In addition, funds can be provided to educational institutions for training and developing researchers.

Intramural Funding

Intramural research capacity in highway safety is limited. NHTSA has a small in-house research staff that analyzes crash data and conducts evaluations of specific safety standards and regulations; the majority of the agency's research funds are contracted out. FHWA has the capacity to support in-house research at its Turner-Fairbank Highway Research Center, but the agency's contract highway safety research program is much larger than its in-house effort. The Injury Control Program of the CDC also has in-house staff with capacity to conduct research, provide technical assistance, and manage the extramural grants program; however, the majority of its funding goes to the grants program.[2] Some state agencies have research departments, but the more common practice is to contract out research projects to universities and consultants.

Extramural Funding

Several methods are available for providing external research funds to individual researchers or research organizations, but not all of these are widely used in the highway safety field.

Contracts

Contracts are generally the preferred method for well-defined research projects in which the desired product can be specified in a detailed manner (Stoto et al. 1988, 414). Solicitation for research is agency-initiated through Requests for Proposals (RFPs) that define the scope of work, often suggest appropriate methodologies for analysis, and specify product requirements in some detail. Outside peer review is generally not involved; rather, agency staff play an active role in evaluating proposals, which must provide detailed cost estimates by task, and in directing the research. Contracts are well suited to applied research in which fundamental research questions have been answered and the purpose is to identify or evaluate different methods of achieving agreed-on goals. However, research that involves solving a specific problem can still require a flexible approach. Both NHTSA and FHWA issue contracts for most of their extramural highway safety research.

Grants

Grants are generally used when problems are not well defined and flexibility is needed to stimulate innovative approaches to advance the state of the knowledge. Grant-supported research is initiated by individual researchers, who prepare applications based on their own ideas that fall within a broad scope of work defined by the agency in Requests for Applications (RFAs) (Stoto et al. 1988, 414). Grant proposals are generally reviewed for scientific merit by outside peers as well as agency staff experts. Agency staff typically do not take an active role in directing the research (the grantee is responsible for managing the research), and research products and costs are less well defined than in a contract arrangement. Grants are well suited for fundamental research in which the objective is often problem identification rather than problem solving. The primary grants program in highway safety is the CDC Injury Control Program.

Cooperative Agreements

A cooperative agreement is a relatively new funding mechanism that falls somewhere between a contract and a grant in terms of flexibility and management of the research (Stoto et al. 1988, 415). Cooperative agreements allow the researcher greater latitude than a contract to define the scope of work and methodological approach, but require a greater degree of specificity than a grant regarding the products to be rendered and the costs to be incurred in performing the research. Cooperative agreements have not been a widely used method of funding highway safety research.

Although research is generally solicited through a formal process, research sponsors can provide for unsolicited proposals from individual researchers on topics that may be of interest. Limited budgets currently preclude encouragement or funding of unsolicited proposals in highway safety research, although agency authorizations allow for funding of unsolicited proposals.

Other Extramural Funding Mechanisms

In addition to contracts, grants, and cooperative agreements, there are several other arrangements that may be used to build and support organizational capacity in priority research areas. For example, CDC provides multiyear grants to university centers to develop programs in injury control. Basic ordering agreements or indefinite-quantity contracts are other commonly used mechanisms to provide research institutions with multiyear funding for a range of tasks under broad areas of research that are spelled out in the basic agreement. Typically, the award is made on the basis of a capability statement, generally for a 2- to 3-year period with one renewal. Specific projects are then defined but a separate bidding and awards process is generally not required for each specific task, streamlining the procurement process. With the exception of the CDC program, there are few multiyear funding arrangements with university or other research centers specializing in various aspects of highway safety research.

Education and Training of Researchers

Research funds can also be used to train and develop researchers. Funds can be provided to universities to develop graduate programs in desired fields and fellowships can be granted to individual students to support graduate education. Although this model has been heavily used in the engineering[3] and scientific communities, it is not common in the highway safety field, in part because of limited funding. Providing incentives for universities to develop highway safety programs or specialties, or even endow chairs, particularly in the fields of engineering, public health, emergency medicine, and behavioral sciences, should go a long way to giving more visibility to highway safety issues in teaching and educational curricula.

Summary

All of these funding mechanisms should be available so that different research needs can be accommodated. However, as is discussed in greater detail in the following sections, the absence or limited use of many of these approaches in funding highway safety research unnecessarily restricts the flexibility needed to stimulate innovation and limits the support required to build strong technical expertise in requisite research disciplines.

INNOVATION AND SCHOLARSHIP

Current methods of conducting highway safety research should be modified in three broad areas to

- Provide more flexibility to stimulate innovation,
- Encourage greater scientific rigor and independence of research, and
- Provide more sustained funding to build research and researcher capacity.

Stimulating Innovation

Broadening the scope of research programs and using more flexible methods of funding research can go a long way to encourage innovative thinking about highway safety issues. For example, grants may be more appropriate than contracts in areas where new approaches are sought because they offer a researcher more latitude to structure a study design that is different from the conventional wisdom. Encouraging investigator-initiated research is another method of stimulating new ideas that may not have been considered in formulating agency research programs. Finally, a simplified and timely procurement process can help ensure that new ideas generated by research are available when needed to inform policy choices and decisions. Although government procurement practices have generally become more constrained with passage of the Competition in Contracting Act and enactment of the Federal Acquisition Regulations (FAR) by the U.S. Office of Management and Budget in 1984, many of these options are available to federal sponsors of highway safety research.

Encouraging Scientific Rigor

The credibility of research results can be enhanced by increasing the scientific rigor and independence of research. Outside peer review of proposals is a well-established mechanism for helping ensure that the proposed scope of research is adequate and the research methodology sound. Not all research projects may require outside peer review, particularly highly applied research projects where the scope of study is relatively narrow and the methodology straightforward, but it should be used when appropriate. Encouraging publication in refereed journals is another way of strengthening the credibility and quality of the research that is conducted and ensuring that the results are widely circulated to the larger research community. Finally, more adequate provision must be made for developing the scientific basis for potentially sensitive automotive regulation, so that a more impartial assessment of the technical merits of government's position versus industry's on proposed regulations can be rendered.

Providing Continuity

Perhaps the most important change needed in the current structure of highway safety research is greater continuity of funding and more attention to building research capacity. Multiyear funding is needed to sustain research in areas that require a long-term effort to realize the benefits of research. The study of injury tolerances in motor vehicle crashes and research on the visual and cognitive capabilities of older drivers are two examples of research that requires considerable analysis and testing before the results can be used to develop specific vehicle crashworthiness or licensing standards. Better mechanisms for defining research priorities and coordinating work among research sponsors with common interests are needed to help focus the agendas and ensure the relevance of long-term research programs. NHTSA, for example, recently brought together a wide range of scientific experts on various aspects of aging in a joint effort with the National Institute on Aging, CDC, and FHWA to help develop a long-range plan for research on the older driver. Such forums, if held on a periodic basis, could provide a means of revising priorities as work progresses and a vehicle for disseminating research that has been completed.

More sustained funding in priority program areas should help attract and retain research expertise in key disciplines to work on highway safety problems. Building adequate programs of research also requires education and training of new researchers through funding of graduate education programs in desired research disciplines and student fellowships.

INSTITUTIONAL STRATEGIES AND OPTIONS

Institutional capability to conduct highway safety research along the lines outlined in the previous section was an issue of great concern to the study committee. Two general strategies were examined: (a) supporting the current primary federal sponsors of highway safety research—NHTSA and FHWA—but with important modifications in the way that these agencies now conduct research, and (b) broadening the research base to tap the research management skills of several organizations, including some who have no current experience in highway safety.

A variety of institutional arrangements were explored, including modifying DOT highway safety research programs, building on the new CDC program, creating a new program in highway safety research at the National Science Foundation (NSF), and creating a new not-for-profit research institute. The pros and cons of each option were evaluated with the following considerations in mind: (a) the priority given to highway safety by the research sponsor, (b) the capacity to conduct research along the lines described in the previous section, and (c) the ability to launch a research program in a timely manner.

Building on Existing Sponsors of Highway Safety Research

Numerous opportunities exist for modifying federally sponsored highway safety research programs to make them more effective. Table 5-1 gives many of the desired characteristics of an innovative research program and indicates whether federal program sponsors currently use these mechanisms.

DOT Programs

DOT has broad authority to conduct highway safety research through a variety of mechanisms that it could use more extensively. The legislation

TABLE 5-1   DESIRED CHARACTERISTICS OF HIGHWAY SAFETY
RESEARCH PROGRAMS AND THEIR CURRENT USE BY FEDERAL
PROGRAM SPONSORS

	Use by Agency		
Characteristic	NHTSA	FHWA	CDC
Grants	No[a]	No[a]	Yes
Contracts	Yes	Yes	No
Investigator-initiated research	No	No	Yes
Outside peer review	No	No	Yes
Multiyear funding of research institutions	No	No	Yes
Mechanisms to define long-term research priorities and programs	No	No	No
Career development	No	No	No

NOTE: NHTSA = National Highway Traffic Safety Administration; FHWA = Federal
Highway Administration; and CDC = Centers for Disease Control.
[a] Technically, NHTSA and FHWA can and have awarded grants. However, they are
administered largely in the same manner as contracts.

authorizing DOT highway safety research and development [23 U.S.C.
Section 403 (a)] provides for a wide range of mechanisms to carry out this
research, including contracts, grants, and research fellowships. Each of
the responsible agencies, NHTSA and FHWA, has its own procurement
office and may enter into arrangements with other federal agencies, state
or local agencies, institutions, or individuals to carry out the research.
"Research" is defined broadly to include, but is not limited to, "vehicle,
highway, and driver characteristics, accident investigations, communications, emergency medical care, and transportation of the injured" [23
U.S.C. Section 307 (d)].

Despite this broad mandate, NHTSA and FHWA view their research
mission more narrowly as supporting specific regulatory and programmatic objectives, for which contracts are the most appropriate funding mechanism (personal communication with the Director of the Office of Contracts and Procurement, FHWA, Sept. 1, 1989).[4]

The heavy reliance on contracting by both NHTSA and FHWA is a
long-term policy. The Dulles Conference of 1979, which focused on
NHTSA's Section 403 research program, remarked on the need for an
"innovative grants" program within the 403 program to support long-term
research that "looks beyond today's problems" (TRB 1979, 40). In 1980
NHTSA did not view this type of research as central to a "mission-
oriented agency . . . (whose) primary objective is to support programmatic research rather than to mount long-term research" (NHTSA 1980, 11).

Today, the leadership of DOT has indicated its desire to create a climate
more conducive to new ideas and new approaches (DOT 1990, 35). The
concern is whether this new climate can be translated into lasting changes,

which include a more sustained commitment to programs of long-term research, greater use of outside peer review to enhance the quality of research, and more flexible funding arrangements to encourage innovation.

CDC Program

The injury control program managed by CDC has many of the desired characteristics to encourage innovation in research. First, it is structured to provide sustained funding in key research areas through multiyear grants to university research centers as well as to individual researchers. The current program provides 3-year support to seven research centers[5] and up to 3-year grants to individual researchers to conduct research in specific program areas (data from Division of Injury Epidemiology and Control, CDC, Oct. 30, 1989).[6] Second, the grants program operates through the traditional peer review grants process, so that the merits of research proposals are judged by the broader academic community as well as by agency staff. Finally, the program has been successful in involving researchers in public health as well as other medical specialists in the study of automotive trauma, thereby providing new perspectives on highway safety problems.

The CDC program received its first permanent funding in FY1989 from the Department of Health and Human Services (HHS) (with a small appropriation by NHTSA), and is at a critical point. Program managers have commenced a regular biannual grants cycle and are in the process of redefining the long-term research agenda.[7] Now that the majority of the funding is provided by HHS rather than NHTSA, however, the priority given to motor-vehicle-related research may not be as strong as in the pilot program when NHTSA provided the majority of the funds.[8] Although motor vehicle crashes are a leading cause of injury, the broad public health perspective of the CDC injury control program extends well beyond the highway safety field. Some highway safety researchers are concerned that the emphasis on highway safety may be weakened by this broadening of perspective.

Potential New Program Sponsors

The committee also examined the potential for developing new institutional arrangements to address the problems it perceived in the current management of highway safety research.

National Science Foundation

One option examined was to develop a new highway safety research program at NSF. A research program with a special emphasis on highway safety could be established within NSF's existing engineering program structure or piggybacked onto its multidisciplinary Engineering Research Centers (ERC) program or both.

A major advantage of developing a research program at NSF is the primacy of research as the agency's mission, which is to sponsor scientific research and support science and engineering education. Its peer review process helps ensure research programs of high academic quality. In addition, the agency has the infrastructure to manage research programs as well as to provide funding to university centers for research and educational support.

Currently, however, there is little program emphasis or staff expertise at NSF in the highway transportation field. The agency now supports between $500,000 and $800,000 in grants under its bioengineering, operations research, and systems analysis divisions that could be considered safety related (personal communication with the Deputy Assistant Director for Engineering, NSF, Oct. 12, 1989). The agency's conditions for developing a new program could also pose a problem. Sponsoring agencies may advise NSF on appropriate priorities for research, but NSF has final control over the agenda and development of the research program. This independence could prove to be a liability if the program is not perceived as relevant by its sponsors.

New Nonprofit Highway Safety Research Institute

Another option examined by the committee was to create a new research institution. The history of the Health Effects Institute (HEI) was reviewed as a possible model.

HEI was created in 1980 as an independent nonprofit corporation and jointly funded by the Environmental Protection Agency (EPA) and the automotive industry to conduct basic research for regulatory purposes on the health effects of vehicle emission standards (GAO 1986, 7). A major purpose of creating HEI was to neutralize the adversarial relationship that had developed between government and industry over environmental regulation; the new institute was to conduct research on regulatory-related issues in a depoliticized scientific environment (Grumbly 1985, 1). A closely associated objective was the improvement of the science base underlying environmental regulation.

Many of the same conditions that led to the establishment of HEI are also present in the highway safety area. The main attraction of creating a new research institute for highway safety along the lines of HEI is the opportunity to start afresh and build research capacity that is relatively independent of the regulatory and political environment.

The obstacles to this approach are several. First, creating a new institution requires strong leadership. HEI had the backing of the Administrator of EPA and the Chairman of General Motors; the institute is chaired by former Special Prosecutor Archibald Cox and his fellow directors, the Presidents of Stanford University and Bell Laboratories (Grumbly 1985, 10–11). It is not evident that similar high-level support for the concept of a highway safety research institute would be forthcoming from DOT or the automobile manufacturers.

Second, sustained commitment is needed to develop a fully operating research organization, and resources must be used initially to create the necessary research infrastructure. In its first 3 years of operation, for example, HEI spent only $1 million, mainly to set up the organization (Grumbly 1985, 31). It was 2 years before any research got under way and 5 years before the institute was operating at nearly full capacity (Grumbly 1985, 31). Lengthy start-up taxes the patience of sponsors and the results-oriented perspective of federal budgeteers.

A final issue is the perceived relevance of the research. Although the sponsors of HEI were strong supporters of its mission to conduct high-quality research, the degree of independence that this implied was difficult to accept in practice. EPA, in particular, was highly critical of the relevance and timeliness of HEI's research agenda, which was perceived as unresponsive to the sponsor's needs (Grumbly 1985, 21).

Given these obstacles, the committee also examined the option of building on HEI rather than creating a new institution. Although this might eliminate start-up concerns, fundamental issues, such as the relevance of the research and the priority given to a new highway research initiative at HEI, remain.

Conclusion

After weighing the options discussed here, the committee (with the exception of one member) concluded that the most workable strategy was to support the existing primary sponsors of highway safety research at DOT, but with certain key changes in the way that any additional funds for research would be used.

There were several reasons for this conclusion. First, highway safety is a mission responsibility for NHTSA and FHWA and these agencies are likely to present a stronger case to Congress for more adequate funding of highway safety research than an agency like NSF or, to a lesser extent, CDC, for which highway safety is not an agency priority. Second, given budgetary realities and the likelihood of obtaining at best relatively small amounts of additional funding, the committee was unwilling to fragment the research effort by spreading the funds. Third, the need to start now to rebuild research capacity to address emerging highway safety problems reduced the desirability of creating new programs or new institutions to conduct highway safety research. Finally, the new leadership and climate at DOT were perceived to be sympathetic to the committee's proposed changes in the way that research programs are currently managed.

The risks of this strategy were evident—DOT's weak track record of supporting quality research and building a cadre of scientific researchers and the difficulty of conducting long-term research in a political environment. One committee member would have preferred a pluralistic approach, allocating a portion of the funds to agencies outside of DOT, but even that member concurred with a substantial increase in resources for the DOT mission agencies. The majority of the committee believed that the wisest course was to concentrate the additional funding in the DOT mission agencies, but only if the funds are allocated by Congress for the purposes detailed in the following section.

RECOMMENDATIONS

Many of the recommendations require modifications in the way that NHTSA and FHWA conduct research. However, there were a few areas in which the committee perceived that more extensive changes were needed to fill major gaps in current research programs.

Rebuilding the Capacity at NHTSA and FHWA To Conduct Long-Term Research

Supporting long-term research at NHTSA and FHWA will require building capacity, encouraging innovative research, coordinating research programs, improving contract research programs, and improving data base support.

Building Capacity

NHTSA and FHWA must do more to develop research capacity in key areas and attract more researchers into the highway safety field. Where programs of long-term research are desired, the agencies should encourage their support by providing multiyear funding of university centers and other research institutions. In addition, the agencies must invest in the future by providing support for graduate programs and research fellowships to ensure that new researchers are being trained in fields of special interest. If additional funds are provided for these activities, these investments can be made without cutting heavily into existing highway safety contract research programs.

Encouraging Innovative Research of High Quality

NHTSA and FHWA should encourage investigator-initiated research proposals and increase the use of more flexible funding instruments, such as grants and cooperative agreements, to encourage innovative approaches to highway safety problems. Outside peer review of research proposals and findings is critical to help ensure high quality and relevance of the research. A set-aside program of small awards (i.e., less than $50,000 per award), modeled on the Strategic Highway Research Program (SHRP) Ideas Deserving Exploratory Analysis (IDEA) program,[9] could also be developed to encourage participation of individual researchers. Finally, federally sponsored projects should include preparation of an article suitable for submission to a refereed journal.

Coordinating Research Programs

The need for improved coordination between NHTSA and FHWA within DOT, and between DOT, CDC, and other sponsors of highway safety research is evident in examining the areas of research required to address emerging safety problems. Joint planning of long-term research agendas would be appropriate to ensure that priority program areas will be adequately addressed. Joint programming of research on topics that cross traditional DOT mission agency responsibilities may also be appropriate. For example, issues such as the effects on safety of new technologies and the aging of the population can best be studied from a systems perspective, which examines the interaction among the human, the vehicle, and the highway. The research agenda-setting process could benefit from a broad examination of similar areas of common interest, so that the systems issues are not overlooked.

Multiyear research plans should also be developed by the DOT mission agencies with input from other appropriate federal agencies, the states, and private industry. Multiyear plans will help define long-term research priorities and provide an agenda for funding and a basis for monitoring progress.

Improving Contract Research Programs

Contract research programs at NHTSA and FHWA could also be strengthened by providing prospective contractors with more advance information on research program priorities, preferably for a 2- to 3-year period. Currently, researchers are provided limited notice of the agencies' research priorities in advance of the annual funding cycle. FHWA provides annual program-level information, which is published in the *Commerce Business Daily* (CBD) in advance of specific RFPs. The RFP is the first notice, however, that researchers receive of NHTSA's research interests. Neither agency publishes longer-range (i.e., 3- to 5-year) research plans or priorities for highway safety, in part reflecting the short-term focus of the research and the changing priorities of the agencies' leadership.

The awards process itself could be improved. Common complaints about both the FHWA and NHTSA contracting processes are their emphasis on cost in selecting among proposals and the length of time for contract award. Both agencies follow a competitive contracting process in which they establish a competitive cost range and then typically award to the lowest fully qualified bidder within this range, although efforts are made during the negotiation process to help assure that the most qualified bidders fall within the cost range. Additional funding should widen the range of qualified research institutions that bid on projects and broaden the scope of inquiry. Shortening the time to award contracts is constrained by the requirements placed by the 1984 FAR on all civilian agency contracting procedures, but there is likely some room for improvement.[10]

Improving Data Base Support

Good data bases provide critical input to programs of long-term research. They provide the grist for analysis of the characteristics of crashes and, over time, provide the basis for monitoring and evaluating the effectiveness of regulations and safety programs.

Highway safety data bases could be improved in several ways. First, better national data are needed on nonfatal crashes, particularly on the injuries sustained in these crashes. Improved hospital records on the incidence of injury by cause (distinguishing motor vehicle from other causes of injury), nature, and severity of injury are critical to this effort (Rice et al. 1989, 33). Second, more adequate data on the characteristics of crashes are needed to support research on crash avoidance. Finally, improved methods of collecting and linking safety data from widely different sources (e.g., police accident reports, hospital records) should be sought. Development of new technologies, such as satellite-based locational referencing systems, and greater automation of data input—both discussed in Chapter 3 in relation to truck safety data—should advance these efforts.

Achieving these improvements, however, is not a simple task. A forthcoming study by TRB, *Data Requirements for Monitoring Truck Safety* (1990), which will recommend data improvements in a single safety-related area, illustrates the complexity of the task. Frequently, the responsibility for data collection is scattered among federal, state, and local agencies, and in some cases, private institutions, each of which has its own objectives in collecting the data. Integrating these needs into a coordinated data system that serves multiple objectives can be a costly endeavor. The recommendations developed in the TRB report will show that solutions are possible, but specifying how these can be accomplished for the data areas mentioned above is beyond the scope of this study.

University Research Centers

Two areas of research—biomechanics and crash avoidance—were singled out for special attention as critical to making further advances in highway safety. A special effort is needed in these fields to ensure an adequate level of funding and to develop a critical mass of researchers. The committee recommended that funding for research in these areas be provided through university research centers, so that the research programs could be directly linked with graduate education to attract and train new researchers.

Biomechanics Research

The federal government should provide multiyear funding to establish one or two centers of excellence to conduct long-term research in biomechanics. Research on population variations and optimization of protection for the various distributions of crash severities and human tolerances to injury is critical to making further advances in injury mitigation and vehicle crashworthiness. The centers should be associated with universities and should expand on existing facilities where possible, so that the majority of the funding can be used for research.

Biomechanics researchers themselves acknowledge that injury biomechanics research is a "science . . . in its infancy" (Viano et al. 1989, 413). Common problems are the lack of trained scientists and engineers with background and experience in the mechanics and physiology of trauma, little development of faculty or curricula to produce new researchers, and absence of funding for long-term research (Viano et al. 1989, 413).

Developing a comprehensive long-term research program in bio-mechanics also requires access to expensive and sophisticated laboratory and testing equipment, such as crash test facilities and impact sleds, as well as the capability to undertake laboratory testing with anesthetized animals and human cadavers. Such facilities are expensive to establish and maintain, and for this reason injury biomechanics, unlike virtually any other research subspecialty in highway safety, needs a focused and concentrated program in one or two university centers.

Although funding for facilities, equipment, and operating personnel should be concentrated, use of these facilities should be open to industry, government, and academic researchers alike on a competitive basis. Outside peer review of research proposals and findings will be critical to ensure research of high quality. Adequate provision should also be made for education and training of new researchers.

The most critical ingredient to a successful long-term research program in biomechanics is sustained funding. With an adequate level of resources and a long-term commitment that should attract new talent to the field, a more extensive science base for motor vehicle safety improvements that better match real-world conditions can be developed.

Crash Avoidance Research

Although vehicle crashworthiness and occupant protection systems can be advanced further, crash investigations suggest that for a significant number of fatal crashes the outcome could not be avoided by any known crashworthiness technology (Viano 1988, 428). Even with vehicle designs that are optimized for injury reduction, severe crashes will continue to result in death and serious injuries. Reducing these deaths and serious injuries requires avoiding crashes altogether through such measures as control of impaired driving, speed enforcement, and use of crash avoidance and warning technologies.

The federal government should provide multiyear funding to establish three to five centers of excellence in crash avoidance research. Although there is less need to concentrate the research as in biomechanics, the number of centers should be limited to allow each to have adequate funds to support an excellent program of research. Programs of human factors and behavioral research as well as research in other disciplines related to driver-vehicle interaction and the role of new technologies in crash avoidance should be central to an expanded initiative in crash avoidance. Research proposals and findings should be peer reviewed and provision made for education and training of new researchers. At the level of funding recommended in this report, all of the additional resources should be used for research and not to support major equipment investment such as a national advanced driving simulator. An expanded commitment to crash avoidance research should help realize emerging opportunities for crash prevention.

New Cooperative Program for State-Sponsored Research

States sponsor a considerable amount of highway safety research (see Table 2-2) and have the potential to do more, particularly on driver- and vehicle-related issues. State highway safety professionals are closest to the problems and are thus in an excellent position both to define appropriate topics for research and evaluation and to use research results. As managers of many highway safety programs and initiatives, they need good research to guide implementation efforts.

The largest current funding source for state-sponsored research on highway safety is the Highway Planning and Research (HP&R) funds. Not surprisingly, these are used primarily to study highway-related and traffic safety issues. However, states may also apply to NHTSA for Section 403 funds for safety research projects and may use Section 402 funds for demonstration and evaluation activities.[11] States may also use their own funds to finance safety research projects.

Although the potential for state-sponsored safety research projects is large, research funds are now spread widely.[12] States have unique problems that warrant individual state studies, but they also share common interests for which pooling of funds and joint research would be more appropriate. For example, in the next several decades all states will face the issue of a growing population of aging drivers and the pressures to develop licensing procedures and educational programs targeted at this population.

One way to encourage more attention at the state level on highway safety research in general and on the opportunities for pooled research in particular would be to create a cooperative program for highway safety research. A mechanism already exists for pooling highway funds for research on highway-related safety topics, the National Cooperative Highway Research Program (NCHRP); a similar mechanism could be created whose focus would be entirely safety related, a National Cooperative

Highway Safety Research Program (NCHSRP). The program could be managed in the same way as NCHRP, that is, by the American Association of State Highway and Transportation Officials in cooperation with DOT and the National Academy of Sciences. In this case, NHTSA as well as FHWA should be involved in determining the research agenda. Input should also be provided by associations representing motor vehicle and law enforcement officials. One of the primary objectives of the NCHSRP would be to involve state-level highway safety professionals, such as administrators and law enforcement officials, in the definition of appropriate research projects on now relatively neglected driver- and vehicle-related issues.

SUMMARY

Meeting the highway safety challenges of the future requires a forward-looking, innovative research program of high quality. Several measures are suggested for restructuring existing research programs to create a climate more conducive to this objective. New initiatives are recommended where a special effort is warranted. Perhaps the most important requirement is a more sustained commitment of resources to support long-term programs of research.

NOTES

1. For example, the Transportation Systems Center (TSC) of the U.S. Department of Transportation, which once had a large human factors group working on alcohol and other highway safety-related issues, now has a small staff working mainly on aviation and maritime issues (personal communication with the Associate Director for Research and Analysis, TSC, Sept. 18, 1989).
2. Approximately 20 percent of CDC's 1989 appropriation was for intramural research and technical assistance (personal communication with the Director, Division of Injury Epidemiology and Control, August 17, 1989).
3. A major goal of the Engineering Research Centers program, a joint National Science Foundation and industry program whose primary purpose is to stimulate multidisciplinary engineering research and development enterprise in the United States, is the development of graduate and undergraduate education programs in cross-disciplinary research (NRC 1988, 7).
4. More flexible funding mechanisms are used, such as cooperative agreements and grants, but typically with states rather than with individual researchers. FHWA also uses a level-of-effort contract through which it purchases the services of a contractor for a specified period for a task that is generally less well defined than in a regular contract (personal communication with the Director, Office of Contracts and Procurement, FHWA, Sept. 1, 1989).
5. The seven injury prevention centers funded by the CDC grants program are University of Alabama, Birmingham; Harvard School of Public Health; Uni-

versity of California at Los Angeles and at San Francisco; Harborview Medical Center; School of Public Health, University of North Carolina; and the School of Hygiene and Public Health, Johns Hopkins University.

6. For FY1990, CDC has organized its research program according to the three phases of injury: prevention, acute care, and rehabilitation. The disciplines of epidemiology and biomechanics may be applied in addressing each of the three major areas.

7. The agenda of the initial 3-year pilot program closely followed the recommendations made in the study by the National Academy of Sciences that provided the impetus for the program (NRC 1985).

8. In the 3-year pilot program, 52 percent of the $22.5 million available to the injury prevention research centers and for individual research grants was spent on motor vehicle–related research. In the first award of permanent funds in FY1989, 37 percent of the $29 million available to the centers and for individual grants was earmarked for motor vehicle–related research. However, 50 percent of the $8.4 million backlog of approved, but unfunded, individual grants was motor vehicle related. Determination of whether research was motor vehicle related or not was made by CDC staff.

9. The SHRP-IDEA program solicits proposals for good ideas in a broad subject area and provides small ($50,000 to $60,000) 1-year funding to individual researchers to develop their idea.

10. Currently FHWA reports a 6-month minimum from the time an RFP is advertised in the CBD to the date of award; NHTSA reports an average of 8 to 9 months for the same process (personal communication with the Directors, Office of Contracts and Procurement, FHWA and NHTSA, Sept. 1 and 7, 1989).

11. According to the legislation, 402 funds can be used for research-related activities, that is, for demonstration programs and for evaluating measures for reducing crashes [23 U.S.C. Section 402 (a) and (c)]. However, the majority of funds are currently spent for developing and operating safety programs.

12. Of the estimated $9.6 million for safety-related projects financed with HP&R funds in FY1988, only $859,000, or 9 percent, was for NCHRP projects (personal communication with the budget analyst, Turner Fairbank Highway Research Center, Sept. 15, 1989).

REFERENCES

ABBREVIATIONS

DOT	U.S. Department of Transportation
GAO	General Accounting Office
NHTSA	National Highway Traffic Safety Administration
NRC	National Research Council
TRB	Transportation Research Board

DOT. 1990. *Moving America: New Directions, New Opportunities.* Feb.

GAO. 1986. *Air Quality Standards: The Role of the Health Effects Institute in Conducting Research.* RCED-86-177BR. Washington, D.C., June, 44 pp.

Graham, J.D. 1989. *Auto Safety: Assessing America's Performance.* Auburn House Publishing Company, Dover, Mass., 253 pp.

Grumbly, T. 1985. *The Health Effects Institute: A New Approach to Developing and Managing Regulatory Science.* Unpublished manuscript, 36 pp.

NHTSA. 1980. Report to the Senate Appropriations Committee on the Transportation Research Board's 403 Program Recommendations contained in Unpublished Report 16 (*Highway Safety Research, Development and Demonstration: Conference Proceedings*). U.S. Department of Transportation, May.

NRC. 1985. *Injury in America: A Continuing Public Health Problem.* National Academy Press, Washington, D.C., 164 pp.

NRC. 1988. *The Engineering Research Centers and Their Evaluation.* National Academy Press, Washington, D.C. 10 pp.

Rice, D.P., E.J. MacKenzie, and Associates. 1989. *Cost of Injury in the United States: A Report to Congress.* Institute for Health and Aging, University of California, San Francisco; Injury Prevention Center, Johns Hopkins University, Baltimore, Md.

Stoto, M.A., D. Blumenthal, J.S. Durch, and P.H. Feldman. 1988. Federal Funding for AIDS Research: Decision Process and Results in Fiscal 1986. *Review of Infectious Diseases,* Vol. 10, No. 2, March–April, pp. 406–419.

TRB. 1979. *Highway Safety Research, Development, and Demonstration: Conference Proceedings.* Unpublished Report 16. National Research Council, Washington, D.C., Dec., 129 pp.

TRB. 1990. *Special Report 228: Data Requirements for Monitoring Truck Safety.* National Research Council, Washington, D.C.

Viano, D.C. 1988. Limits and Challenges of Crash Protection. *Accident Analysis and Prevention,* Vol. 20, No. 6, Dec., pp. 421–429.

Viano, D.C., A.I. King, J.W. Melvin, and K. Weber. 1989. Injury Biomechanics Research: An Essential Element in the Prevention of Trauma. *Accident Analysis and Prevention,* Vol. 22, No. 5, pp. 403–417.

6

Funding Requirements

Conducting the research identified in this study to anticipate and attack the highway safety problems of the future will require a more adequate level of funding and a more sustained commitment of resources than in the past decade. Additional funding should be dedicated to programs of long-term research to provide the knowledge base for making further advances in highway safety. This expanded program of research should provide benefits that far outweigh the costs.

LEVEL OF FUNDING

Current annual federal and state funding of approximately $70 million supports highway safety research that is largely focused on the short-term mission objectives of its sponsors and the maintenance of supporting data bases. Research in support of agency activities is a legitimate and necessary use of funds; highway safety data bases are an essential tool for research and program management and monitoring. However, at current funding levels, there are few additional resources available to support long-term programs of research on issues that may emerge as safety problems in the future or to grapple adequately with persistent safety problems.

Long-term programs of research are most effectively sponsored and coordinated at the national level where issues of national significance can be identified and targeted for funding. The federal government typically funds research that is long term and fundamental in nature. To support this activity, additional annual federal funding of $30 million to $40 million (in 1990 dollars) should be provided, growing at 5 to 7 percent annually in real terms as capacity develops over a 5- to 10-year period. This recommended funding level would be higher but for the lack of available qualified scientists to conduct the research.

This recommended increase in federal funding reflects the committee's collective judgment that research spending should be greater than at pre-

130

sent, but must be tempered initially by the lack of capacity to absorb a large funding increase. A 50 percent increase in current annual public funding, or $30 million to $40 million, was judged to be a reasonable starting point. This level of funding should provide a more adequate level of research spending on highway safety relative to other major public health problems and more adequate resources to address long-term programs of research.

The additional funds recommended here should be used to rebuild the capacity of the primary federal sponsors of highway safety research at the U.S. Department of Transportation (DOT)—the National Highway Traffic Safety Administration (NHTSA) and the Federal Highway Administration (FHWA)—to conduct programs of long-term research. Such programs should emphasize peer-reviewed, investigator-initiated research, multiyear funding of research programs, and associated educational programs to build research capacity in key disciplines. A portion of these funds should be dedicated to establishing one or two university centers of excellence in biomechanics research and three to five centers in crash avoidance research. DOT should monitor the use of the additional funds for these purposes and should also attempt to evaluate the benefits of new research sponsored by these funds.

The committee recognizes the important contribution of the Injury Control Program of the Centers for Disease Control (CDC) in involving the public health and medical community in the study of automotive crash trauma and the role of acute care and rehabilitation in injury mitigation. The committee supports a continuing CDC program emphasis on motor-vehicle-related injuries as the leading single cause of fatal injuries (Rice et al. 1989, 11).

Finally, the committee advocates a new cooperative program for state-sponsored highway safety research. Funding would be provided by broadening the eligible use of existing federal highway safety funds and requiring state matching funds.

SOURCES OF FUNDING

Additional funds for long-term research programs should be provided in the upcoming congressional reauthorization of NHTSA's and FHWA's safety research budgets in the Highway Safety Act and the National Traffic and Motor Vehicle Safety Act. The two primary sources of federal funds for these programs are the highway trust fund and general appropriations. Because the trust fund is reauthorized for a 4-year period, a set-aside of additional trust fund revenues for highway safety research offers greater assurance of sustained funding than the annual appropriations process. Thus, to the extent possible, additional funding should be provided from trust fund revenues. Any shortfall in trust fund revenues from obligation ceilings should be made up from general revenues.

Given current constaints on the federal budget, funds to support a new cooperative program for state-sponsored highway safety research should come from greater use of existing federal research funds for state research projects and leveraging of additional state matching funds. Federal Section 403 funds can now be used for state-sponsored research projects, and 402 funds should also be made available for this purpose.[1] Specifically, research should be defined as an eligible use of federal 402 funds in reauthorizing legislation. Congress should be amenable to this change, because research is critical to the development of effective safety programs, and the federal government would have a role in coordinating the research as it does now in the management of the National Cooperative Highway Research Program (NCHRP). State funds should be required to match federal dolllars in the proposed new cooperative program for highway safety. The required match, however, could be waived where joint state research is proposed, as in the NCHRP program, to encourage pooling of research funds on topics of common interest.

BENEFITS OF EXPANDED HIGHWAY SAFETY RESEARCH PROGRAM

An expanded program of research to support the activities suggested in this study should provide a level of effort more commensurate with the size of the highway safety problem. Current annual federal and state funding for highway safety research of approximately $70 million represents one-tenth of 1 percent of the $70 billion in medical expenses, lost wages, and property damage associated with motor vehicle crashes each year.

Even if current spending were doubled, however, highway safety research would remain underfunded relative to other major public health problems, such as cancer and heart disease. Motor vehicle crashes result in an equivalent number of early deaths but do not receive nearly the same level of funding for research (Figure ES-1). Hence, oppportunities for reducing early deaths from motor vehicle crashes may not be fully exploited. Moreover, the potential for reducing loss extends beyond saving lives. Motor vehicle crashes are responsible for injuries that frequently require costly medical care and may involve permanently disabling brain and spinal cord injuries as well as extensive property damage.

Unlike many other public health problems, where a single breakthrough like the development of a new drug or a vaccine can result in a major savings in lives, there is no single highly effective countermeasure that will bring comparable gains in highway safety. Rather, progress is more likely to come from small advances through a wide range of safety interventions. The role of research is to identify and evaluate the most promising of these measures.

The benefits of an expanded effort to pursue these opportunities more aggressively are almost certain to outweigh the costs. Although it is not possible to quantify the benefits precisely, small incremental gains can produce large savings, given the size of the problem. Perhaps equally important, research can provide the knowledge to make more effective investment decisions. The costs of requiring a new motor vehicle safety standard or upgrading a segment of highway to improve safety are substantial. Research can help ensure that these investments are made wisely to achieve the maximum safety gains.

NOTE

1. The diversion of 402 funds from safety program operations to research would likely be small. In FY1990, highway traffic safety grant (i.e., 402 fund) authorizations were nearly $131 million (U.S. Congress 1990, 105).

REFERENCES

Rice, D.P., E.J. MacKenzie, and Associates. 1989. *Cost of Injury in the United States: A Report to Congress.* Institute for Health and Aging, University of California, San Francisco; Injury Prevention Center, Johns Hopkins University, Baltimore, Md.

U.S. Congress. House. Committee on Appropriations. 1990. Department of Transportation and Related Agencies Appropriations Bill, 1991. Report 101-584. 101st Congress, Second Session.

Appendix A

Historical Overview of Highway Safety Research Programs and Priorities

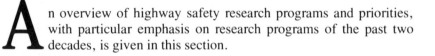n overview of highway safety research programs and priorities, with particular emphasis on research programs of the past two decades, is given in this section.

ORIGINS OF HIGHWAY SAFETY RESEARCH

The field of highway safety research grew with the expansion of the nation's highway system and the rapid increase in automobile use. The evolution of research in the safety field is traced before and after the legislation of the 1960s, which expanded the federal role.

Research Before the 1960s

Highway-related safety research has the longest tradition. The Federal Highway Act of 1921 authorized the first federal aid for highway research and the Hayden-Cartwright Act of 1934 laid the foundation for state-sponsored highway planning and research activities from a set-aside of federal apportionments (FHWA 1976, 321).[1] Although the main focus of early research was on materials and surfaces to support road-building activities, highway safety became an issue as early as 1924 when then-Secretary of Commerce Herbert Hoover held a National Conference on Street and Highway Safety (TRB 1979, 3). The Bureau of Public Roads of the U.S. Department of Commerce, with the support of the American Association of State Highway Officials, published the *Manual on Uniform Traffic Control Devices for Streets and Highways* in 1935. In 1937 the Bureau submitted studies to Congress dealing with, among other

134

topics, the need for uniform traffic laws and vehicle inspection to reduce traffic crashes (FHWA 1976, 343; TRB 1979, 3). Highway-related safety research, however, remained largely decentralized at the state level until the expansion of the federal role in highway safety in the 1960s.

Most early highway safety initiatives focused on the driver as the major contributor to motor vehicle crashes. However, the emphasis was less on research than on education. Safety campaigns, driver training programs, and driver licensing requirements were established to train safe drivers and pedestrians (Eastman 1984, 122). It was not until the 1950s with the emergence of a new discipline, human engineering, that psychologists began to conduct fundamental research on the driving task and the basic skills required of drivers (FHWA 1976, 349). Behavioral research became more sophisticated in the early 1960s as researchers examined the perceptual environment faced by motorists on high-speed roadways and studied such issues as road tracking, speed sensing, car following, overtaking and passing, object avoidance, sign reading, and path finding (FHWA 1976, 349).

Because of the dominant focus on the driver as the primary cause of crashes, vehicle crashworthiness research remained a largely undeveloped field until the 1950s. The first efforts to examine the role of the vehicle in crash injuries came from the work of Hugh DeHaven, whose studies of survivability in airline crashes in the 1930s and 1940s were applied to motor vehicle crashes (National Committee for Injury Prevention and Control 1989, 120). During this time, a handful of medical researchers— Straith, Woodward, and Stapp—also began to examine the causes and mechanisms of injury in automobile crashes and concluded that many injuries could be prevented by designing automobiles for crash protection (Eastman 1984, 192). In the 1950s, the pace of crash injury research quickened, boosted by the support of the Society of Automotive Engineers, the American Medical Association, the American College of Surgeons, and finally the insurance industry, which sponsored several research projects on vehicle crashworthiness at Cornell University (National Committee for Injury Prevention and Control 1989, 121).

At the same time, the automobile manufacturers began to examine the safety aspects of vehicle design and to conduct limited crash testing and laboratory research on vehicle improvements to reduce crash injury (Eastman 1984, 222–233). In the mid-1950s the Ford Motor Company developed and marketed specific safety features to improve occupant protection; these included seat belts, improved door locks, padded dashboards, and energy-absorbing steering wheels. Safety research, however, had a limited effect on occupant protection design for the motor vehicle fleet as a whole until the federal government began to regulate minimum safety performance standards.

Expansion of the Federal Role

The rise in motor vehicle fatalities and the death rate (measured in fatalities per 100 million vehicle miles traveled) during the 1960s began to draw Congressional attention to the need for an expanded federal role in highway safety. The U.S. Department of Commerce had provided Congress with a review of *The Federal Role in Highway Safety* in 1959. Numerous Congressional hearings on automobile safety followed, most notably the investigative hearings of Senator Ribicoff. In 1965, publication of Ralph Nader's *Unsafe at Any Speed* raised public consciousness of the issue of highway safety (Flink 1975, 215–216).

These efforts resulted in legislation—the National Traffic and Motor Vehicle Safety, and the Highway Safety, Acts of 1966—significantly expanding the federal role in highway safety and creating the National Highway Safety Bureau (NHSB), the precursor of the National Highway Traffic Safety Administration (NHTSA), to assume these new responsibilities.

The legislation also brought a new focus to research. A federal program of highway safety research was authorized as an integral part of the legislation mandating federal regulation of motor vehicle safety standards and state and local highway safety programs; separate funding was provided through Section 403 of the Highway Safety Act. The purpose of the program was to conduct research to provide technical support for regulation and, more generally, to advance the knowledge base in highway safety (TRB 1979, 4).

The first director of the NHSB, William Haddon, is well known for his matrix (Haddon 1979, 47), which provided a framework for organizing research programs and countermeasure development on the principal factors contributing to crashes (see text box). The 1966 Arthur D. Little study of *The State of the Art of Traffic Safety* reinforced the need for a broad understanding of the complex factors, which interact to affect the safety of the highway transportation system. Over the next 20 years, research was conducted on each of the principal factors affecting highway safety—the human, the vehicle, and the highway.

DRIVER AND PEDESTRIAN RESEARCH SINCE THE 1960s

The Highway Safety Act of 1966, which required the federal government to establish uniform standards for state highway safety programs, provided the impetus for a companion research and demonstration program to improve the knowledge base on human factors affecting safe driving.

The Haddon Matrix

| | Factors | | |
Phases	Human	Vehicle	Physical and Socioeconomic Environment
Precrash			
Crash			
Postcrash			
Results	Damage to People	Damage to Vehicles and Equipment	Damage to Physical Environment and Society

SOURCE: Adapted from Haddon 1979, 47.

NHTSA and Other Federally Sponsored Research

In the U.S. Department of Transportation (DOT), NHTSA has been the chief sponsor of driver-related[2] and cosponsor with the Federal Highway Administration (FHWA) of pedestrian-related safety research during the past two decades. Spending and program activity peaked during the mid-1970s with large multiyear programs in alcohol and pedestrian research (Table A-1). The major research priorities of the 1970s are described in the following sections.

Alcohol Research

Alcohol-impaired driving was identified as a problem of major proportions and concern early in DOT's history. A 1968 Report to Congress by the Secretary of Transportation (U.S. Congress 1968) documenting the available research linking alcohol use to highway crashes created widespread interest in mounting a comprehensive attack on this national problem. Encouraged by strong congressional support, the agency quickly developed plans to assist states and communities in strengthening their programs to reduce alcohol-impaired driving.

Initial research attempted to develop a better understanding of the problem by looking at the effects of alcohol on driver performance in laboratory studies. Whereas previous efforts had focused on the convicted driver, in the mid-1970s research was initiated on a general deterrence approach within the driving population by increasing the driver's risk of detection, apprehension, and sanction. Field studies were carried out to determine the effectiveness of various enforcement strategies and court

TABLE A-1 NHTSA APPROPRIATIONS FOR DRIVER AND PEDESTRIAN SAFETY RESEARCH BY PROGRAM CATEGORY, FY1972–1989

Program Area	Appropriation ($ thousands) by Fiscal Year																			Total
	1972	1973	1974	1975	1976	TQ	1977	1978	1979	1980	1981	1982	1983	1984	1985	1986	1987	1988	1989	
Alcohol and drug research[a]	1,700	2,200	2,200	2,200	1,895	500	1,795	1,750	1,488	950	541	850	850	1,050	960	1,534	1,574	1,468	1,443	26,948
Driver and pedestrian factors																				
Occupant protection	NA	NA	600	310	305	0	295	265	255	500	560	1,150	1,150	1,195	1,200	1,077	1,250	1,214	1,725	13,051
Driver education and training	NA	NA	308	275	410	0	123	232	0	98	283	0	0	0	0	0	0	0	0	1,729
Driver licensing and control	NA	NA	476	445	575	0	401	420	307	409	382	0	0	0	0	0	0	0	0	3,415
Motorcycle safety	NA	0	0	275	450	0	373	250	192	356	289	0	0	0	0	0	0	0	0	2,185
Older driver research	0	0	0	100	40	0	140	0	223	0	0	0	0	0	40	0	0	0	315	858
Pedestrian and bicycle safety	0	NA	490	795	970	0	1,000	834	802	667	486	0	0	0	0	0	0	0	10	6,054
Speed and other unsafe driving actions	0	NA	126	450	550	825	468	399	383	620	751	200	150	0	0	0	0	368	525	4,990
Subtotal	800	1,838	2,000	2,650	3,300	825	2,800	2,400	2,162	2,650	2,751	1,350	1,300	1,195	1,240	1,077	1,250	1,582	2,575	35,745
Grand total	2,500	4,038	4,200	4,850	5,195	1,325	4,595	4,150	3,650	3,600	3,292	2,200	2,150	2,245	2,200	2,611	2,824	3,050	4,018	62,693

NOTE: Figures represent budget appropriations and are not adjusted for reprogramming actions that occurred. They do not include NHTSA staffing and administrative costs. TQ = Transition Quarter. NA = Breakdown not available.

[a] Breakdown between alcohol and drug research not available; 15 to 20 percent of total estimated for research on drugs other than alcohol.

sanctions, tests were devised to enhance the reliability of police detection of driver impairment, and testing and evaluation of breath test measurement devices and vehicle ignition interlock systems were conducted.

Pedestrian Research

Another important field of study during the 1970s was the pedestrian research program, which began with a pioneering study (Snyder and Knoblauch 1971) that examined approximately 2,000 urban pedestrian crashes in 13 large cities across the country. Seven major crash types were identified, which became the research targets for the 1970s. (This crash-typing methodology was also applied to crashes involving bicyclists and motor vehicles.) Countermeasures were developed for each crash type, which included training programs, public information and educational materials, and model traffic safety regulations. Limited field testing was conducted and more extensive multiyear demonstration projects were performed for the most promising approaches. Finally, evaluation studies were conducted to examine the cost-effectiveness of countermeasures, such as those directed toward children (Blomberg et al. 1978; Berger and Dueker 1980; Blomberg et al. 1983).

Research To Support Driver Education and Licensing

NHTSA's early program activities also involved research related to driver-oriented programs administered by state and local governments, such as driver education and training and driver licensing. The purpose of the research, which received fairly steady support throughout the 1970s (Table A-1), was to provide results that would have practical application in state and community program operations.

NHTSA's research in driver education concentrated on basic educational programs for the novice driver. Research needs in driver education were identified in a planning effort in the late 1960s, which included a driving task analysis, development of instructional objectives and curriculum specifications, identification and development of training devices and off-street procedures, and development of knowledge and skill tests and testing procedures. These efforts culminated in a major demonstration program initiated by NHTSA with the DeKalb County School System in Georgia in 1976 to determine the crash reduction potential of high school driver education programs. In the final report (Stock et al. 1983), which compared students who had participated in an extensive model training program and a more modest standard training program with a control group who had received no formal instruction, no statistically significant differences were found in the number of crashes and violations between teenage students who had received training and a control group who had not.[3] Other studies, funded by the Insurance Institute for Highway Safety (IIHS) (Robertson 1980; Lund et al. 1986), found that the availability of high school driver education programs causes students to become licensed earlier, increasing their exposure at an earlier age.

NHTSA's research program on driver licensing concentrated on the development of driver screening techniques and procedures, knowledge and skill tests and testing procedures, driver improvement and control activities, and a graduated licensing system for novice drivers. On the basis of the agency's recommended classified license system, research has produced driver manuals, knowledge tests, off-street skill tests, and on-street tests for motorcycle, passenger vehicle, and heavy vehicle license applicants. In 1977 NHTSA developed a model system for provisional or graduated licensing of novice drivers (Croke and Wilson 1977), which was based on a review of federal and state research and state practices. NHTSA and the American Association of Motor Vehicle Administrators recently developed recommendations for an improved driver-entry system for young novice drivers (Tannahill and Smith 1990).[4]

Other Program Areas

NHTSA's remaining research funds during the 1970s were allocated among studies on occupant protection, speeding and other unsafe driving actions, and motorcycle safety (Table A-1).

Early studies in occupant protection focused on determining why the majority of drivers and passengers refused to use safety belts. Based on findings from these studies, research was undertaken to improve the comfort and convenience of belt systems and educational materials were developed and tested on special target populations. Public opinion surveys on airbags and the concept of state laws mandating belt use were also conducted. In 1977 the first in-traffic surveys of general seat belt use in 19 cities were begun. Since 1983 these surveys have been conducted yearly at an annual cost of about $300,000.

Initial research on speeding stemmed from early motor vehicle crash causation studies that identified human error as a major contributing factor (Perchonok 1972, Sabey 1973). Speeding was identified as a factor in 33 percent of fatal crashes, and other unsafe driving actions (e.g., tailgating, running a red light or stop sign, cutting into traffic), in 26 percent of these crashes (Lohman et al. 1976). Preliminary research was carried out to identify driver motivations for a number of the most frequently occurring unsafe driving behaviors. When the 55-mph national speed limit went into effect in 1973, research was directed toward the development of performance guidelines for radar speed-measuring devices. New automated speed enforcement technologies were also identified and evaluated.

NHTSA's motorcycle safety research program concentrated on three major areas: operator testing and licensing, education, and helmet use. Research was also conducted on conspicuity enhancement, alcohol use, and moped safety.

NHTSA Driver and Pedestrian Research Programs Since 1981

The change in administration in 1981 resulted in a substantial reduction in federal funding for driver- and pedestrian-related research (Figure 2-2) and a concentration of research activities in two areas—occupant protection and alcohol abuse (Table A-1).

Issuance of the final rule on passive restraints (FMVSS 208) in 1984 gave considerable impetus to the enactment of state laws mandating safety belt use by adults[5] and rekindled interest in research on safety belt promotion and development of effective state safety belt use laws. The impacts of enforcement, media programs, adjudication outcomes, and employer programs in fostering increased belt use were studied.

Alcohol research in the 1980s continued to analyze the effectiveness of various general deterrence strategies, such as checkpoints and use of roadside sobriety tests, as well as countermeasures to address alcohol-impaired driving among younger drivers. Each of these two program areas—occupant protection and alcohol—is currently funded at less than $2 million.

In 1988 and 1989, increases of $200,000 and $1 million, respectively, in NHTSA's driver and pedestrian research budget permitted a broadening of the research agenda. Concern about mobility and safety of the aging stimulated renewed interest in NHTSA's extensive work in pedestrian safety and some earlier research on older drivers. Increasing the speed limit on rural Interstates rejuvenated research on speed monitoring, enforcement, and crash impacts. Continued emphasis on alcohol research is likely as long as alcohol-impaired driving remains a major factor contributing to motor vehicle fatalities. In comparison, except for specific studies of ways to encourage safety belt use, research on occupant protection is not as likely to receive the attention that it has in the past.

Other Federally Sponsored Research

The Injury Control Program administered by the Centers for Disease Control (CDC) has provided some new resources for driver-related research under the category of injury prevention. Research grants have been awarded for studies on prevention of alcohol-impaired driving and prevention of childhood injury through measures to increase bicycle helmet and safety belt use among children.

State and Private Research

Funding of research on driver- and pedestrian-related safety issues outside of NHTSA and CDC is limited. A few states conduct research on driver-related issues. For example, the California Department of Motor Vehicles has a long history of research on the relationship between driver characteristics and crash involvement.

Private sponsorship of driver-related research is limited. IIHS has conducted studies on various driver-related issues. The automobile manufacturers have conducted limited research on the relationship between driver behavior and traffic safety (U.S. Congress 1989, 1036).

Summary Assessment

Research on driver- and pedestrian-related safety issues has not received the level of funding of other safety research areas (Figure 2-2). Today, NHTSA's driver and pedestrian research program represents less than 15 percent of the agency's total research budget. CDC, the states, and the private sector contribute modest additional resources.

What research has been done, primarily at NHTSA, has focused on two areas—alcohol and occupant protection. Together they have received nearly two-thirds of the funds available for behavioral research since the inception of NHTSA's research program (Table A-1). A large share of the research funds expended by NHTSA over the last two decades has been devoted to what may be characterized as program development or evaluation, often with a short-term focus. For example, many of the studies in the alcohol program in recent years are short-term projects, evaluating a specific countermeasure or developing products that will support state and local alcohol programs that the agency is encouraging. These short-term research needs are legitimate, but they have made it difficult to develop and execute a coherent long-term research program.

Emerging issues, such as the problems of the older driver and pedestrian and driver reactions to new technologies, have renewed interest in research on driver- and pedestrian-related issues. As advances are sought, particularly in the area of crash avoidance, research on the human element in highway safety—on a more sophisticated understanding of the interaction among the driver, the vehicle, and the highway—may be given a higher priority than it has received in the past (Campbell 1989, 8).

VEHICLE SAFETY RESEARCH SINCE THE 1960s

Passage of the highway safety legislation of 1966 reflected a national mood for action. The authorizing legislation for NHTSA (originally the National Highway Safety Bureau) called upon it to develop regulations to make vehicles safer. With a mandate to act, NHTSA issued 29 motor vehicle safety standards and proposed 95 more within 2 years of its creation (Graham 1989, 32). Many of these early safety standards were based on the judgment of safety experts or on the recommended practices of the Society of Automotive Engineers (Kahane 1984). Following this initial round of safety standards, NHTSA began investing in research on motor vehicle safety. The agency's major ongoing programs of research are in crashworthiness, biomechanics, and crash avoidance.

NHTSA Research To Support Rulemaking

Crashworthiness

The first director of the National Highway Safety Bureau, William Haddon, Jr., a physician from New York State, was noted for his interest in highway crashes as a public health problem. He recognized the potential for large safety gains from improved protection of vehicle occupants from the devastating consequences of the "second collision" between the occupants and the inside of the vehicle.[6]

Recognizing that half of motor vehicle fatalities involve frontal collisions, NHTSA's initial crashworthiness research program emphasized mitigation of frontal injuries. The agency adopted a "technology forcing" strategy with its early emphasis on airbags (Graham 1989). However, with this exception and the technology thrust of the Experimental Safety Vehicle Research Program (described later), NHTSA has generally conducted research in support of safety performance standards, leaving it to industry to develop appropriate products to meet the standard. For this reason, much of NHTSA's research has focused on developing anthropometric test devices (crash dummies) and appropriate injury criteria and funding crash tests to determine the performance of both dummies and alternative vehicular designs to meet safety standards.

After the initial emphasis on mitigation of frontal collisions, research attention shifted during the mid-1970s to mitigation of side impacts. In

1988, after roughly 10 years of development, NHTSA proposed its amended side-impact standard (see discussion below on biomechanics).

In recent years, NHTSA's crashworthiness research has focused more on rollover crashes. A rollover crash device was developed that pitches vehicles over laterally after they first develop momentum by advancing down a track. The tests are intended to help improve understanding of the tendency of different models to roll, once tripped, and will examine how roof crush may affect injury during a rollover collision (Digges 1987). The test results are also intended to help improve simulations of vehicle rollover.

Biomechanics

NHTSA-funded efforts in biomechanics support agency rulemaking by developing criteria by which to measure the safety performance of new cars. Research in biomechanics, that is, the study of injury mechanisms and human tolerances to crash impacts, provides the basic knowledge to support the development of injury criteria and testing devices and, from these, to devise performance standards for testing vehicle crashworthiness.

During the early years, NHTSA-sponsored research drew on previous biomechanical research conducted by or sponsored by General Motors. After several years this research resulted in performance standards based on acceleration measured at the head and chest and loads measured at the femurs of crash dummies. These performance standards are used to assess the occupant protection provided by new model cars in 30-mph frontal barrier crashes.

Research funded by NHTSA on trauma from side impacts has led to a proposed amended regulation on side impacts (*Federal Register* 1988). The research unfolded over several years, beginning with problem analysis and then moving to cadaver testing at different impact speeds and ultimately to injury criteria and dummy development (Eppinger et al. 1984). The results of the cadaver tests were used to relate crash impacts, as measured by acceleration, to the probability of injury. This information, in turn, was used to develop a side-impact dummy. Industry researchers, however, have criticized DOT's acceleration-based test criteria and the test dummy developed on the basis of these criteria as poor predictors of soft organ damage and overall injury probability in side-impact crashes (Viano et al. 1989a, 1989b; GMRL 1989).

Crash Avoidance

Research in crash avoidance is inherently more difficult than in crashworthiness because of the complex interaction of the driver, the vehicle, and the environment in potential and actual crashes. Although excellent data sources have been developed for analyzing crash severity over the last two decades, little information on precrash factors is available to help isolate vehicle characteristics that might have contributed to a crash.

In the past, insights on crash avoidance have come largely from special in-depth studies on a sample of vehicles involved in crashes. The results of all of these studies (see Chapter 2) show that driver error or failures are contributing factors leading to crashes in roughly 60 to 90 percent of the cases. The studies indicate that vehicle failures alone play a relatively minor role. Further improvements in most individual vehicle features are likely to result in only incremental improvements in crash avoidance, unless they somehow provide better information to drivers more quickly.

Crash avoidance research has traditionally taken a secondary role in NHTSA's motor vehicle safety research program, funded at slightly more than half the level of crashworthiness research. Over the years NHTSA research in this area has focused on technology (e.g., improved lighting, especially brake lighting), improved tire and brake performance, and some funding for development of radar braking and warning devices. Small projects have been funded to develop performance standards for mirrors, headlights, and vehicle conspicuity.

As in the crashworthiness area, rollover research is a current priority. NHTSA's primary approach to this issue is the development of simulation models.

Among the larger current research efforts is a demonstration program of the reliability of antilock brakes on large truck-tractors. The current field test, which is evaluating the performance of 200 trucks equipped with antilock brakes with a comparison group, is a roughly $3.5 million, multi-year effort, and is the largest single program in NHTSA's crash avoidance research budget.

A small amount of crash avoidance research is addressing an emerging technology, referred to as the intelligent vehicle-highway system (IVHS), to assess its potential for reducing traffic congestion and enhancing safety. NHTSA is participating in a project to test the use of radar systems to maintain headways in a semiautomated traffic environment (NHTSA's funding is $100,000). The agency is also providing small grants for seed money in IVHS research efforts (about $100,000) and participating in efforts to assess the potential safety and efficacy of IVHS (about $425,000).

Summary

The total expenditure of NHTSA research funds to support rulemaking is relatively modest, about $13 million annually.[7] Approximately $8 million is spent on crashworthiness and biomechanics. Major projects currently include the rollover studies discussed earlier, continued work in side impacts, and improved frontal protection. About $2 million of the $8 million is for biomechanics research, specifically for developing improved crash dummies and better head injury criteria. About $5 million of NHTSA's motor vehicle safety research program is devoted to crash avoidance. These funds are spread over issues such as heavy-truck handling, stability, and braking performance; light truck, van, and multipurpose vehicle rollover simulations; headlight performance models; performance evaluation tools for rear lighting and mirror systems; prototype development for advanced vehicle warning systems, and seed money for current IVHS efforts.

Other NHTSA Research Programs

Experimental Safety Vehicle Research

The Experimental Safety Vehicle Research Program was a major feature of NHTSA's research effort during the agency's first decade. The research program, based on a specific section of NHTSA's authorizing legislation [P.L. 89-563, Sec. 106(a)2], began in 1968 with the goal of demonstrating new designs in occupant protection and crash avoidance features. In the early 1970s the goal was restated to demonstrate that automobiles could be built that would protect occupants in high-speed frontal and rollover crashes without requiring active restraints while at the same time meeting federal emission standards and conserving fuel (Mannella 1975). NHTSA's emphasis on demonstrating new technology in this program was similar to the technology thrust of the research programs at the Urban Mass Transportation Administration, Federal Railroad Administration, and National Aeronautics and Space Administration.

The program, later restructured and dubbed the Research Safety Vehicle (RSV) Program, was not directly linked with proposed rulemaking. Instead, it was designed to test concepts that might ultimately be regulated by NHTSA (Finklestein and Stephenson 1979). Several domestic and international manufacturers produced prototype research safety vehicles for evaluation and testing. The RSV program—a 7-year, $30 million research effort—demonstrated many effective occupant protection and crash avoidance concepts, such as more comfortable safety belts, automatic belts, emergency tensioning retractors, airbags, and antilock braking systems. Some of these innovations were added to production vehicles without being specifically required. The steering and handling capabilities of the experimental minicar RSV, however, fell short of the requirements of production vehicles (Richardson 1982), and the program was ended in the early 1980s.

Evaluation of Vehicle Standards

Beginning in 1975, NHTSA began formally evaluating its motor vehicle safety standards (Kahane 1984). A small team of researchers in the Office of Program Evaluation was assigned responsibility. This effort received renewed impetus in 1981 by an executive order requiring all federal agencies to evaluate proposed and existing regulations. Several of the agency's existing motor vehicle safety standards have been reviewed and found effective, for example, standards requiring side marker lamps, energy-absorbing steering columns, high-penetration-resistant windshields, head restraints, and center high-mounted stoplights (Kahane 1984, 1989). Although NHTSA originally relied on contract research to support its evaluations, it has increasingly performed its evaluations with a small agency staff.

Injury Control

Beginning in 1985, NHTSA collaborated with CDC in a 3-year pilot program to substantially improve and upgrade the federal support for injury control research (NRC 1988). Automobile crash injuries account for the largest proportion of injury-related morbidity and mortality (NRC 1985). Because its research program is directly linked with its regulatory responsibilities, and because of the small size of its program, NHTSA has had little opportunity to fund injury control research and has had little success fostering an interest in automotive trauma research within the medical research community.

For this program, NHTSA provided the bulk of the funds for the $26 million pilot effort (U.S. Congress 1989, 845), and CDC set up and administered a review process for awarding research grants. NHTSA also reviewed and commented on grant applications. Because of NHTSA's interest in biomechanics, one of the five injury prevention research centers established in the pilot program, Wayne State University, focused on biomechanics. Slightly more than half of the individual research grants ($8.4 million) were directed to projects directly related to automotive crash trauma, although a much smaller number dealt with vehicle-related research issues (personal communication with Assistant Director for Extramural Research, Center for Environmental Health and Injury Control, CDC, April 5, 1990).

When the successful pilot program was completed, Congress funded a permanent injury control program under the CDC in 1989, with the majority of the funding from the Department of Health and Human Services. As a result, NHTSA funds were freed for other research, and the direct link between CDC and NHTSA was severed.

Private Research

Although NHTSA's vehicle-related research program is probably small compared with that of private industry, relatively little information about private expenditures for research is in the public domain. The bulk of private research is devoted to product development, such as vehicle structural improvements and occupant restraint systems. As the automotive industry has become worldwide, the research has followed suit. For example, some recent innovations in occupant safety, such as child safety seats and safety belts integrated into the passenger seat, have been developed by Volvo and BMW (IIHS 1989b).

Two major exceptions to the focus of private safety research on product development in the United States are worth noting, however. The three biggest automobile manufacturers combined probably spend more than NHTSA on research in crashworthiness and biomechanics. GM's program is undoubtedly the largest because of the size of GM Research Laboratories and its numerous contributions to vehicle safety design and peer-reviewed scientific publications (GMRL 1988). Many current vehicular safety features, such as energy-absorbing steering columns, originated at GM.

The second major exception is the funding provided by the insurance industry to IIHS, which has an annual budget of $8 million and funds some projects on vehicle-related safety research. In comparison with the emphasis on product development by the automobile manufacturers, research at IIHS is focused more on the analysis of crash results. For example, a major project begun during 1988 will collect extensive information on driver injury in crashes from the Charlottesville, Virginia, metropolitan area to help identify vehicle design changes that could reduce injuries (IIHS 1988).

Summary Assessment

The technology for reducing harm in frontal collisions has been identified and advanced in many areas: head restraints, energy-absorbing steering columns, deforming steering wheels, windshield glazing and antilacerative laminated windshields, airbags, safety belts, and child restraints. The standards set for these vehicle features are improving the crashworthiness of new model cars. Each year the New Car Assessment Program 35-mph barrier crash tests show reduced average scores on test dummies (Hackney et al. 1989). The benefits of NHTSA's safety standards, when analyzed separately and in combination, have outweighed the costs (Kahane 1984, 1989; Crandall et al. 1986). The technical research issues, in terms of current standards, address continued incremental improvements in performance.

Research in crash avoidance is lagging behind technology development in private industry. Considerable manufacturer interest currently is devoted to developing advanced displays that take advantage of new technology or technology newly adapted to the automobile. For example, the "head-up" display is designed to project essential information that appears outside the windshield near the front of the hood; this display is already being offered in special models.

Innovations such as the head-up displays and radar warning systems may provide safety benefits; they may reduce driver error or inattention, and thereby reduce the major contributing cause of crashes. Too much new information for the driver, however, could also be distracting. In the longer run, advanced technology integrating vehicles with the roadway could also reduce driver error. This research area could have substantial safety benefits and is likely to become a major priority for future funding. An expanded program of human factors research is needed to evaluate the potential benefits and costs of these and other advanced technologies (Finkelstein 1989).

HIGHWAY-RELATED SAFETY RESEARCH SINCE THE 1960s

FHWA Research

Following the passage of the Highway Safety Act of 1966, FHWA assumed explicit responsibility and received funding (through Section 403) for research in four safety areas: identification and surveillance of crash locations; highway design, construction, and maintenance; traffic engineering services; and pedestrian safety (shared with NHTSA). Since 1970, much of the research sponsored by FHWA has centered on four areas of highway safety: roadside safety, large-truck safety, traffic engineering, and wet weather crashes. Taken together, these four areas have accounted for more than half of all FHWA-sponsored safety research spending (TRB staff estimate based on Annual Progress Reports of the

Federally Coordinated Program of Highway Research, Development, and Technology).

Roadside Safety

Roadside crashes have long been considered a serious safety problem. Collisions with fixed objects along the sides of roadways—trees, poles, barriers, buildings, ditches, and embankments—account for about 30 percent of all fatal crashes and result in 10,000 to 15,000 deaths annually (IIHS 1989a; NHTSA 1989, 5–7).

Roadside safety first became a priority of FHWA's when it was discovered that the massive sign supports being erected on early segments of Interstate highway were posing serious hazards to motorists who had run off the road. Starting in the mid-1960s, FHWA sponsored several studies to develop improved designs for breakaway sign and luminaire supports, roadside recovery zones, and protective guardrails and barriers (Texas Transportation Institute 1967; Roy Jorgensen Associates 1966).

Since 1970, FHWA has spent nearly $15 million on research aimed at improving roadside safety (TRB staff estimate based on Annual Progress Reports of the Federally Coordinated Program of Highway Research, Development, and Technology). Over the years, the agency has tested and evaluated the performance of numerous kinds of crash cushions, breakaway supports, and longitudinal barriers, often using both crash test results and crash data (Viner and Boyer 1973; White and Hirsch 1974; Kimball et al. 1976). More recently, this research has led to breakaway designs for utility guy wires, performance standards for bridge rails, and modified guardrails and barriers capable of handling heavy buses and large trucks (Hirsch and Arnold 1981; Bronstad 1987).

Large-Truck Safety

Completion of large segments of the Interstate highway system during the 1960s resulted in major productivity gains for the trucking industry, which were followed by increased truck traffic and gradual increases in the average size and weight of trucks.

Recognizing that over time substantial changes had taken place in the size, mix, and volume of trucks on the highways, FHWA first began sponsoring large-truck safety research in the mid-1970s. Early FHWA work in this area included studies of crash data for single-trailer and double-trailer combinations and full-scale testing and simulation to determine the effect of increased truck size and weight on vehicle handling and stability (Vallette et al. 1981; Hanscom 1980). Findings from these studies were examined closely during the debate over the potential safety effects of the more liberal truck size limits that were established as part of the Surface Transportation Assistance Act of 1982.

Other results from FHWA truck safety studies have included a system for providing truck drivers with a safe descent speed on steep grades, identification of the causes of single-vehicle truck crashes on interchange ramps, and guidelines for the designation of routes for transporting hazardous materials (Johnson et al. 1982; Urbanek and Barber 1980).

Most recently, an FHWA-sponsored investigation of the adequacy of highway design criteria for large trucks has led to revisions in the American Association of State Highway and Transportation Officials' *Policy on Geometric Design of Highways and Streets,* providing guidance to local highway engineers on modifying curve and intersection design where substantial large-truck traffic is projected (Harwood et al. 1990).

Traffic Engineering

Since the late 1960s, FHWA has spent almost $10 million and published more than 50 reports on a variety of traffic engineering topics ranging from railroad-grade crossings and speed control to traffic signs and pavement markings (TRB staff estimate based on Annual Progress Reports of the Federally Coordinated Program of Highway Research, Development, and Technology).

Traditionally, FHWA traffic engineering research has supported the *Manual on Uniform Traffic Control Devices* (MUTCD), and thus has often addressed specific traffic engineering problems. For example, in the mid-1970s, concerned that an aging and more heavily traveled highway system would require increasingly more maintenance and rehabilitation in hazardous high-traffic areas, FHWA sponsored several studies to improve traffic control devices and procedures at construction work zones (Graham et al. 1977; Humphreys et al. 1979; McGee and Knapp 1978). Results of these studies included the preparation of a report on breakaway barricades and a two-volume supplement to the MUTCD, which led to greatly expanded use of concrete median barriers, new and better arrow boards, and improved practices for work-zone traffic control (Freedman 1985; Jenning and Demetsky 1983).

Most recently, even more specific FHWA studies have addressed guidelines in the MUTCD and other traffic engineering manuals for curve warning signs, traffic signal brightness, and traffic control devices at left-turn lanes.

Wet Weather Accidents

During the 1970s, FHWA undertook a comprehensive 10-year, $10 million effort in cooperation with the states to develop a better understanding of wet weather crashes (TRB staff estimate based on Annual Progress Reports of the Federally Coordinated Program of Highway Research, Development, and Technology). Accomplishments of the program included the development of more skid-resistant materials, better techniques for measuring and inventorying the skid resistance of pavement surfaces, and improved methods for applying antiskid treatments. As a result of these efforts, highway engineers now have a better understanding of hydroplaning and the need for good drainage, although they still lack systematic procedures for determining exactly when and where antiskid treatments are cost-effective to apply.

Other Safety Research

In contrast to the major research areas just discussed, several FHWA projects have been initiated that have received only sporadic support—often because they lacked either strong advocacy among staff or clear potential for short-term pay-off. Examples of these projects include efforts to improve pedestrian and bicycle safety, to develop cost-effectiveness evaluation techniques for highway safety management, and to devise safer and more cost-effective highway design criteria.

Safety Research Programs Since 1981

Since 1981 FHWA's research budget has been reduced by one-third from the level it had received during the 1970s. Research funds have been concentrated on selected high-priority, short-term problems (High Priority National Program Areas) that were intended to be solved in 3 to 5 years. Areas of current attention include development of a Highway Safety Information System (see Chapter 2), reflectivity of traffic control signs and pavement markings, highway safety improvements for the older driver, and determination of cost-effective design options for different types of highways. Additional projects on revised geometric design criteria for large trucks and work-zone traffic control represent continuations of existing programs.

Proposed Safety Research for the 1990s

FHWA is planning a far more ambitious research agenda for the 1990s, particularly if new funding for research is made available in the reauthorizing legislation for the highway program in 1991. Like NHTSA, FHWA would place greater emphasis on human factors research to identify and understand incompatibilities between driver capabilities and limitations (fatigue, age) and highway design (intersections, freeway interchanges). As part of this effort, FHWA would also examine the potential of new communications technologies, such as real-time roadside messages and in-vehicle navigation displays, to warn drivers of impending potentially hazardous highway conditions without information overload. The joint interests of FHWA and NHTSA in these areas suggest the need for greater coordination between the agencies' highway safety research programs than in the past.

State Research

State highway and transportation departments spend more than twice as much as FHWA each year on highway safety research (Table 2-2). Projects are financed primarily by federal Highway Planning and Research (HP&R) funds.

States are closest to highway system operating problems, and therefore are in a good position to test and evaluate traffic signals, raised pavement markers, barrier systems, and the many other safety-related products that have been introduced over the years. In 1988, for example, nearly one-fourth of the 82 safety-related HP&R studies were efforts to evaluate the performance of roadside safety hardware (data provided by the FHWA Office of Research, Development, and Technology).

In most cases, state research has been aimed at correcting unique local problems associated with each state's own traffic and roadway conditions, although in recent years, some states have assembled the staff and facilities to handle research on large national problems that affect many states. As might be expected, larger states like California, New York, and Texas have the most diverse research programs. These states are frequently under contract to FHWA and are important participants in nationally coordinated research projects. The kinds of safety studies currently being performed by states range from an investigation of twin trailer truck crashes (Washington) to the testing of bridge rail design (Louisiana) and the development of roadside crash rates for rural two-lane highways (New York).

Because the costs of some research projects may be large and the benefits may be national in scope, states have created a way to pool their HP&R funds—the National Cooperative Highway Research Program (NCHRP). Since the NCHRP was established in 1962, about 80 projects have been completed in highway safety. Because the goal of the NCHRP is to focus research on specific problems that are amenable to quick-action responses, these projects are typically 1- to 3-year efforts. For example, a safety-related project that is currently in progress is a 3-year, $450,000 effort to improve traffic control and barrier treatments for work zones.

Private Research

Highway-related research in the private sector is concerned primarily with product development. Among the safety areas that have received the most attention by private industry are the development of roadside safety hardware and the improvement of nighttime visibility of signs and pavement markings. Past research accomplishments include the General Motors roadside improvement program of the 1950s and 1960s (General Motors 1977), which studied energy-absorbing guardrails, ditch contours, and breakaway sign supports, among other improvements; design and testing of concrete barrier systems by General Motors during the 1970s; development of reflective sign and pavement marking materials by the 3M Company; and evaluation of wood-post guardrails by the timber industry. Frequently, private-sector researchers have tried to improve upon products that were first generated through government research. For example, extensive federal and state funding of research in control of snow and ice during the 1970s led to the discovery of the deicing chemical calcium magnesium acetate, which has since been refined and marketed in a more usable form by the Chevron Chemical Company.

Summary Assessment

Broad participation of the federal government, states, and private companies in highway-related safety research over several decades has brought many advances in highway design and roadside improvements. The greatest progress has been made in those areas where specific problems have been identified and research has developed practical solutions that can rapidly be put into practice, such as devices to protect motorists from roadside hazards. Many of these technologies are now well known and well tested; the issue that remains is identifying under what situations they can be most cost-effectively employed.

By comparison, an area of highway-related safety research that has probably advanced the least over the past 30 years is the development of a comprehensive understanding of how roadway geometric features affect safety. For nearly 50 years researchers have tried to measure the effects of various lane and shoulder widths, side slopes, and alignments on safety, yet, despite these efforts, few widely accepted models of the safety effects of individual geometric features have been established, and even less is known about the combined effects of several features (TRB 1987, 78–79). Researchers have questioned the safety rationale for such basic driver information systems as signs, pavement markings, and traffic signals (Council and Cirillo 1988, 44–46) and the basis for many safety-related engineering decisions, such as the choice of design vehicles for intersections and obstacle heights for designing vertical curves, which in many cases are based on guidelines that were set long ago by the consensus of standards committees (Hauer 1988, 243–244). In part, these gaps in knowledge reflect research programs that have emphasized applied, short-term results.

Emerging safety issues, such as the safety implications of new IVHS technologies, will place a higher priority on research that addresses fundamental safety relationships. Fully understanding the effects of new technologies on different driver subgroups and the interaction among the driver, the vehicle, and the highway in crash avoidance will require not only a new level of coordination between the research programs of FHWA and NHTSA, but a renewed emphasis on programs of long-term research.

NOTES

1. Research was specifically identified as an eligible activity in the Federal-Aid Highway Act of 1944; the Federal-Aid Highway Act of 1962 restricted the $1\frac{1}{2}$ percent set-aside for research and planning purposes only (FHWA 1976, 321).
2. The information on NHTSA's programs was provided by the Office of Driver and Pedestrian Research.
3. Preliminary results from a follow-up evaluation of the DeKalb study, which tracked the control and experimental groups through 6 years of driving experience, indicated a significant difference in the number of crashes and violations between those students who had received some minimum training and the control group (Smith 1987, 4). However, there were no significant differences in the number of crashes between those students who had received extensive training and the control group.
4. The comprehensive driver-entry system advocated by NHTSA and the American Association of Motor Vehicle Administrators includes the following features: (*a*) learner's permit; (*b*) parent-supervised driving practice, including nighttime driving; (*c*) nighttime restriction except for supervised driving; (*d*) a legal drinking age of 21 and zero blood alcohol concentration for underage drivers; (*e*) mandatory safety belt usage by all vehicle occupants; (*f*) no crashes or convictions within a specified time; (*g*) prompt restrictions after crashes or convictions; and (h) a distinct provisional license (Tannahill and Smith 1990, 19).

5. The rule required a phase-in of passive restraints starting with 1987 models, but also included a recision provision stating that if states representing two-thirds of the nation's population enacted mandatory safety belt use laws before April 1, 1989, the requirement for automatic protection would be removed (Graham 1989, 180). An insufficient number of states passed laws that met minimum DOT requirements by the required deadline.
6. There is also a "third collision" between soft tissue and skeletal structures that takes place inside the body itself as it is being stopped by the vehicle interior or restraint system (Viano 1987, 3).
7. This figure does not include NHTSA staff support or other administrative costs.

REFERENCES

ABBREVIATIONS

FHWA	Federal Highway Administration
GMRL	General Motors Research Laboratories
IIHS	Insurance Institute for Highway Safety
NHTSA	National Highway Traffic Safety Administration
NRC	National Research Council
TRB	Transportation Research Board

Arthur D. Little, Inc. 1966. *The State of the Art of Traffic Safety.* C-67770. Cambridge, Mass., June, 624 pp.

Berger, S.S., and R.L. Dueker. 1980. *Experimental Field Test of Proposed Anti-Dart Out Training Programs,* Volumes 1–3. Applied Science Associates, Inc., Valencia, Pa., Dec., 461 pp. NTIS: PB-83-112656, PB-83-112664, PB-84-158419.

Blomberg, R.D., A. Hale, and D.F. Preusser. 1978. *Experimental Field Test of the Model Ice Cream Truck Ordinance in Detroit.* Dunlap and Associates, Inc., Norwalk, Conn., April, 109 pp. NTIS: PB-283419.

Blomberg, R.D., A. Hale, W.A. Leaf, and D.F. Preusser. 1983. *Experimental Field Test of Proposed Pedestrian Safety Messages,* Volumes 1–3. Dunlap and Associates, Inc., Norwalk, Conn., Nov., 194 pp. NTIS: PB-84-211572, PB-84-211580, PB-84-211598.

Bronstad, M. 1987. *Bridge Rail Designs and Performance Standards.* Report FHWA-RD-87-049. FHWA, U.S. Department of Transportation.

Campbell, B.J. 1989. A Call for Behavior Research. *Highway Safety Directions,* Vol. 1, No. 4, Winter.

Council, F., and J. Cirillo. 1988. Current Status of Research and Implementation. *In Highway Safety: At the Crossroads* (R. Stammer, ed.), American Society of Civil Engineers, New York, N.Y.

Crandall, R., H. Gruenspecht, T. Keeler, and L. Lave. 1986. *Regulation of the Automobile.* The Brookings Institution, Washington, D.C., 202 pp.

Croke, J., and W. Wilson. 1977. *Model System for Provisional (Graduated) Licensing of Novice Drivers.* HS-802-313. Teknekron, Inc., Washington, D.C., NHTSA, U.S. Department of Transportation, April, 165 pp.

Digges, K. 1987. *Light Truck Safety Research in NHTSA.* SAE Technical Paper

871099. Society of Automotive Engineers, Warrendale, Pa.

Eastman, J.W. 1984. *Styling vs. Safety.* University Press of America, Inc., Lanham, Md. 280 pp.

Eppinger, R., J. Marcus, and R. Morgan. 1984. *Development of Dummy and Injury Index for NHTSA's Thoracic Side Impact Research Program.* SAE Technical Paper 840885. Society of Automotive Engineers, Warrendale, Pa.

Federal Register. 1988. Vol. 53, No. 17, Jan. 17, pp. 2,239–2,260.

FHWA. 1976. *America's Highways: 1776–1976.* U.S. Department of Transportation.

Finkelstein, M., and R. Stephenson. 1979. Status Report of the United States. Presented at the 7th International Technical Conference on Experimental Safety Vehicles. U.S. Department of Transportation, pp. 21–27.

Finkelstein, M. 1989. Future Motor Vehicle Safety Research Needs: Crash Avoidance. Presented at the 12th International Technical Conference on Experimental Safety Vehicles, Gothenburg, Sweden.

Flink, J.J. 1975. *The Car Culture.* The MIT Press, Cambridge, Mass., 260 pp.

Freedman, M. 1985. *Traffic Signal Brightness.* Report FHWA-RD-85-005. FHWA, U.S. Department of Transportation.

General Motors. 1977. *Half a Century and a Billion Kilometers Safely.* UC 346. Milford, Mich., Nov.

GMRL. 1988. Safety Research at the General Motors Research Laboratories: Examining the Causes and Control of Automotive Crashes and Injury. *Search,* Vol. 23, No. 3, July–August.

GMRL. 1989. Side-Impact Protection: GM Tackles the 'Next Safety Frontier.' *Search,* Vol. 24, No. 3, July–August, 8 pp.

Graham, J. 1989. Auto Safety: *Assessing America's Performance.* Auburn House Publishing Co. Dover, Mass.

Graham, J.L., R.J. Paulsen, and J.C. Glennon. 1977. *Accident and Speed Studies in Construction Zones.* Report FHWA-RD-77-88. FHWA, U.S. Department of Transportation.

Hackney J., W. Hollowell, and D. Cohen. 1989. Analysis of Frontal Crash Safety Performance of Passenger Cars, Light Trucks, and Vans and an Outline of Future Research Requirements. Presented at the 12th International Technical Conference on Experimental Safety Vehicles, Gothenburg, Sweden.

Haddon, W., Jr. 1979. Options for the Prevention of Motor Vehicle Crash Injury. In *Proceedings of the Conference on the Prevention of Motor Vehicle Crash Injury,* Ben-Gurion University of the Negev, Beersheba, Jan. 10, pp. 45–65.

Hanscom, F.R. 1980. *The Effect of Truck Size and Weight on Accident Experience and Traffic Operations,* Volume II: *Traffic Operations.* FHWA, U.S. Department of Transportation.

Harwood, D.W., J.M. Mason, W.D. Glauz, B.T. Kulakowski, and K. Fitzpatrick. 1990. *Truck Characteristics for Use in Highway Design and Operation,* Volume I: *Research Report.* Report FHWA-RD-89-226. FHWA, U.S. Department of Transportation.

Hauer, E. 1988. A Case for Science-Based Road Design and Management. In *Highway Safety: At the Crossroads* (R. Stammer, ed.), American Society of Civil Engineers, New York, N.Y.

Hirsch, T.J., and A. Arnold. 1981. *Bridge Rail to Restrain and Redirect 80,000 lb Trucks.* Report FHWA-TX-81/16. FHWA, U.S. Department of Transportation.

Humphreys, J.B., H.D. Maulten, and T.D. Sullivan. 1979. *Identification of*

Traffic Management Problems in Work Zones. Report FHWA-RD-79-4. FHWA, U.S. Department of Transportation.

IIHS. 1988. *The Year's Work 1988.* Arlington, Va.

IIHS. 1989a. *IIHS Facts 1989.* Arlington, Va.

IIHS. 1989b. *Status Report* (Washington) (Special Issue: *Designing Safer Vehicles*), Vol. 24, No. 8.

Jenning, B., and M. Demetsky. 1983. *Evaluation of Curve Delineation Signs on Rural Highways.* Report FHWA-VA-84-16. FHWA, U.S. Department of Transportation.

Johnson, W.A., R.J. DiMarco, and R.W. Allen. 1982. *The Development and Evaluation of a Prototype Grade Severity Rating System.* Report FHWA-RD-81-185. FHWA, U.S. Department of Transportation.

Kahane, C. 1984. *The National Highway Traffic Safety Administration's Evaluations of Motor Vehicle Safety Standards.* SAE 84092. Society of Automotive Engineers, Warrendale, Pa.

Kahane, C. 1989. *An Evaluation of Center High Mounted Stop Lamps Based on 1987 Data.* Report DOT-HS-807-442. NHTSA, U.S. Department of Transportation, July.

Kimball, C.E., M.E. Bronstad, J.D. Michie, J.A. Wentworth, and J.G. Viner. 1976. *Development of Collapsing Ring Bridge Railing System.* Report FHWA-RD-76-39. FHWA, U.S. Department of Transportation.

Lohman, L.S., E.C. Leggett, J.R. Stewart, and B.J. Campbell. 1976. *Identification of Unsafe Driving Actions and Related Countermeasures.* Report DOT HS-807-064. NHTSA, U.S. Department of Transportation, Dec.

Lund, A.K., A.F. Williams, and P. Zador. 1986. High School Driver Education: Further Evaluation of the DeKalb County Study. *Accident Analysis and Prevention,* Vol. 18, No. 4, pp. 349–357.

Mannella, G. 1975. Research and Development in Future Automobile Regulation. In *Proceedings, Fourth International Conference on Automotive Safety,* U.S. Department of Transportation, pp. 455–486.

McGee, H.W., and B.G. Knapp. 1978. *Visibility Requirements of Work Zone Traffic Control Devices.* Report FHWA-RD-78-143. FHWA, U.S. Department of Transportation.

National Committee for Injury Prevention and Control. 1989. *Injury Prevention: Meeting the Challenge.* Oxford University Press, New York, 303 pp.

NHTSA. 1989. *Fatal Accident Reporting System 1988.* Report DOT HS-807-507. U.S. Department of Transportation, Dec.

NRC. 1985. *Injury in America: A Continuing Public Health Problem.* National Academy Press, Washington, D.C., 164 pp.

NRC. 1988. *Injury Control: A Review of the Status and Progress of the Injury Control Program at the Centers for Disease Control.* National Academy Press, Washington, D.C., 77 pp.

Perchonok, K. 1972. *Accident Cause Analysis.* Cornell Aeronautical Laboratory, Inc., Ithaca, New York, July.

Richardson, F. 1982. Results of the United States Research Safety Vehicle Program. In *Proceedings, Ninth International Technical Conference on Experimental Safety Vehicles.* U.S. Department of Transportation.

Robertson, L.S. 1980. Crash Involvement of Teenaged Drivers When Driver Education is Eliminated from High School. *American Journal of Public Health,* Vol. 70, No. 6, June, pp. 599–603.

Roy Jorgensen Associates. 1966. *Evaluation of Criteria for Safety Improvements on the Highway.* U.S. Bureau of Public Roads, Washington, D.C.

Sabey, B. 1973. *Accident Analysis in Great Britain.* U.K. Transport and Road Research Laboratory, Crowthorne, Berkshire, Oct.

Smith, M.F. 1987. Summary of Preliminary Results: Follow-Up Evaluation Safe Performance Curriculum Driver Education Project. Presented at the Annual Conference of the American Driver and Traffic Safety Education Association, Spokane, Wash., Aug. 10.

Snyder, M.B., and R.L. Knoblauch. 1971. *Pedestrian Safety: The Identification of Precipitating Factors and Possible Countermeasures.* Volumes 1 and 2. Operations Research, Inc., Silver Spring, Md., Jan., 350 pp., NTIS: PB-197749 and PB-197750.

Stock, J.R., J.K. Weaver, H.W. Ray, J.R. Brink, and M.G. Sadof. 1983. *Evaluation of Safe Performance Secondary School Driver Education Curriculum Demonstration Project.* Report DOT HS-806-568. Battelle Columbus Laboratories, Columbus, Ohio, June.

Tannahill, J., and M. Smith. 1990. States' Experience with Inexperienced Drivers. *Traffic Safety,* Vol. 90, No. 1, Jan./Feb., pp. 18–21.

Texas Transportation Institute. 1967. *Highway Sign Support Structures.* U.S. Bureau of Public Roads, Washington, D.C.

TRB. 1979. *Highway Safety Research, Development, and Demonstration: Conference Proceedings.* Unpublished Report 16. National Research Council, Dec., 129 pp.

TRB. 1987. *Special Report 214: Designing Safer Roads: Practices for Resurfacing, Restoration, and Rehabilitation.* National Research Council, Washington, D.C., 319 pp.

Urbanek, G.T., and E.J. Barber. 1980. *Development of Criteria for Transporting Hazardous Materials.* Report FHWA-RD-80-105. FHWA, U.S. Department of Transportation.

U.S. Congress. House. Committee on Public Works. 1968. *1968 Alcohol and Highway Safety Report.* Committee Print 90-34. Government Printing Office, Washington, D.C.

U.S. Congress. House. Committee on Appropriations. 1989. Department of Transportation and Related Agencies Appropriations for 1990. Hearings. . . 101st Congress, First Session, Part 4.

U.S. Department of Transportation. 1959. *The Federal Role in Highway Safety.* Government Printing Office, Washington, D.C., 232 pp.

Vallette, G.R., H. McGee, J.H. Sanders, and D.J. Enger. 1981. *The Effect of Truck Size and Weight on Accident Experience and Traffic Operations.* FHWA, U.S. Department of Transportation.

Viano, D.C. 1987. *Role of Biomechanics in Vehicle Design for Crash Protection.* GMR-5677. General Motors Research Laboratories, Warren, Mich., Jan. 28, 13 pp.

Viano, D.C., I.V. Lau, D.V. Andrzejak, and C. Asbury. 1989a. Biomechanics of Injury in Lateral Impacts. Accident Analysis and Prevention, Vol. 21, No. 6, Dec., pp. 535–551.

Viano, D.C., I.V. Lau, C. Asbury, A. King, and P. Begeman. 1989b. Biomechanics of the Human Chest, Abdomen, and Pelvis in Lateral Impact. In *33rd Annual Proceedings, Association for the Advancement of Automotive Medicine,* AAAM, Arlington Heights, Ill.

Viner, J.G., and C.M. Boyer. 1973. *Accident Experiences with Impact Attenuation Devices*. Report FHWA-RD-73-71. FHWA, U.S. Department of Transportation.
White, M.C., and T.J. Hirsch. 1974. *Test and Evaluation of Energy Absorbing Barriers*, Volume 1: *Corrugated Steel Pipe Crash Cushions*. Report FHWA-RD-74-14. FHWA, U.S. Department of Transportation.

Study Committee
Biographical Information

A. Ray Chamberlain, *Chairman,* is the Executive Director of the Colorado Department of Highways. He holds a bachelor's degree in engineering from Michigan State University, a master's degree in engineering from Washington State University, and a Ph.D. in engineering from Colorado State University. Dr. Chamberlain was President of Colorado State University, where he held a number of positions, including Dean of Engineering, Executive Vice President, Treasurer, and professor of civil engineering. Before his appointment to the Colorado Department of Highways, Dr. Chamberlain held several executive positions in the private sector as Chief Executive Officer of Chemagnetics, Inc., Executive Vice President of Simons, Li and Associates, and President of Mitchell and Co., Inc. A registered professional engineer, Dr. Chamberlain is a member of the American Society of Civil Engineers. He also serves on the Executive Committee of the Strategic Highway Research Program of the National Academy of Sciences and is a member of the Transportation Research Board (TRB) Committee for the Study To Assess Advanced Vehicle and Highway Technologies.

Richard D. Blomberg is President of Dunlap and Associates, Inc. He received his bachelor's and master's degrees in industrial and management engineering from Columbia University. Mr. Blomberg has directed or been involved in the application of human engineering and systems analytic principles to highway safety at Dunlap and Associates, Inc. since 1968. He has also served as a consultant member and human factors specialist on the Aerospace Safety Advisory Panel of the National Aeronautics and Space Administration since 1987. Mr. Blomberg is a member of the Society of Automotive Engineers, the Operations Research Society of America, and TRB's Committee on Pedestrians.

Noel C. Bufe has served as the Director of the Traffic Institute at Northwestern University and Professor at the Kellogg Graduate School of Management since 1978. He received his bachelor's degree in police administration, his master's degree from the School of Criminal Justice, and his

Ph.D. from the Department of Education at Michigan State University. Before his directorship at Northwestern University, Dr. Bufe served as Deputy Administrator of the National Highway Traffic Safety Administration, as Administrator of the Office of Criminal Justice Programs in the Michigan Department of Management and Budget, and as Michigan's first Governor's Highway Safety Representative. Dr. Bufe's professional affiliations have included Vice President for Traffic Safety and Board Executive Committee member of the National Safety Council, Board Member of the National Commission Against Drunk Driving, and Presidential Appointee to the National Highway Safety Advisory Committee of the U.S. Department of Transportation. Dr. Bufe received the National Safety Council's Distinguished Service to Safety Award in 1988.

John D. Graham is an Associate Professor of Policy and Decision Sciences at the Harvard School of Public Health and Deputy Director of the New England Injury Prevention Research Center. Dr. Graham received his bachelor's degree in economics and politics from Wake Forest University, his master's in public affairs from Duke University, and his Ph.D. in public policy analysis from Carnegie-Mellon University. He was Senior Staff Associate of the Committee on Risk and Decision Making at the National Research Council and Project Manager of Unregulated Mobile Source Emissions at the Health Effects Institute. Dr. Graham recently served as a member of TRB's Study Committee To Identify Measures That May Improve the Safety of School Bus Transportation.

Trevor O. Jones is Chairman of the Board of Libbey-Owens-Ford Company, a manufacturer of automotive glass, and President of the International Development Corporation of Cleveland, Ohio, a private consulting firm. He received degrees in electrical engineering from Aston Technical College in Birmingham, England, and in mechanical engineering from Liverpool Technical College. Mr. Jones began his engineering career at General Motors, where he rose to become Director of GM's Proving Grounds. Before coming to Libbey-Owens-Ford, he held several executive positions at TRW Inc., including Vice President of Engineering TRW Automotive Worldwide, Group Vice President and General Manager of TRW's Transportation Electrical and Electronics Group, and Group Vice President of Strategic Planning, Business Development and Marketing for the Automotive Sector. Mr. Jones was appointed to the National Motor Vehicle Safety Advisory Council in 1971, and became vice chairman in 1972. In 1975 he was appointed to the National Highway Safety Advisory Committee, and became its first nongovernmental chairman in 1976. He is a member of the National Academy of Engineering and a Fellow of the British Institute of Electrical Engineers, the American Institute of Electrical and Electronic Engineers, and the Society of Automotive Engineers. He has served on numerous committees of the National Research Council.

Lester P. Lamm is president of the Highway Users Federation for Safety and Mobility (HUFSAM). He received his bachelor's degree in civil engineering from Norwich University and undertook postgraduate studies at the Massachusetts Institute of Technology and the University of Maryland. Mr. Lamm came to HUFSAM after a 31-year career with the Federal Highway Administration (FHWA), in which he rose through the ranks to become FHWA's Executive Director and Deputy Administrator. Mr. Lamm is a member of the Board of Governors of the International Public Works Federation, a member of the Subcommittee on Planning and Policy Review of TRB, a Director of the International Road Federation, a Director of the National Commission Against Drunk Driving, an Executive Committee Member of the Strategic Highway Research Program, and a member of the Advisory Board of the Northwestern University Traffic Institute. He is the recipient of the Department of Transportation Secretary's Gold Medal, a Distinguished Federal Executive Award, and the American Association of State Highway and Transportation Officials' Man-of- the-Year Award.

Lester B. Lave is the James H. Higgins Professor of Economics at Carnegie-Mellon University and has been on the Carnegie-Mellon faculty since 1963. Dr. Lave received his bachelor's degree in economics from Reed College and his Ph.D. in economics from Harvard University. He was a consultant with the Rand Corporation in Santa Monica, California, and to the General Motors Research Labs, and then Senior Fellow at the Brookings Institution. Dr. Lave is past President of the Society for Risk Analysis (1985-1986) and a member of the American Economic Association, the American Public Health Association, the American Academy of Arts and Sciences, and the Institute of Medicine. He has been a member of numerous committees of the Research Council and is a Member of the Board on Health Promotion and Disease Prevention of the Institute of Medicine.

Ellen J. MacKenzie is Assistant Director of the Health Services Research and Development Center at The Johns Hopkins University and Associate Professor in the Department of Health Policy and Management, and has joint appointments in the Department of Biostatistics and the Division of Emergency Medicine. Dr. MacKenzie received her bachelor's degree in mathematics from Rutgers University, and her master's degree and Ph.D. in biostatistics from The Johns Hopkins University. She is a member of the Board of Directors of the Association for the Advancement of Automotive Medicine, a member of the American Public Health Association, the American Statistical Association, the Eastern Association for the Surgery of Trauma, and the Association for Health Services Research.

Hugh W. McGee is a consulting engineer and principal in the firm of Bellomo-McGee, Inc. Dr. McGee received his bachelor's and master's degrees and Ph.D. in civil engineering from Pennsylvania State University. Before coming to Bellomo-McGee, Inc., Dr. McGee was a Senior Associate with Alan M. Voorhees and Associates, Inc., a Program Manager at Biotechnology, and a Vice President at Wagner-McGee Associates, Inc. Dr. McGee is a registered professional engineer. His affiliations include membership in the American Society of Civil Engineers, Fellow of the Institute of Transportation Engineers, and member of TRB's Committee on Traffic Control Devices.

Brian O'Neill is president of the Insurance Institute for Highway Safety (IIHS) and the Highway Loss Data Institute (HLDI). He received his bachelor of science in mathematics and statistics from the Bath University of Technology in Bath, England. Before coming to IIHS, he served as Manager of Wolf Research and Development Corporation. Mr. O'Neill has been with the IIHS and the HLDI since 1969, serving in positions of increasing responsibility as Vice President for Research, Senior Vice President, and Executive Vice President of IIHS, and Senior Vice President of HLDI. Mr. O'Neill is a member of the American Public Health Association, the American Statistical Association, the Royal Statistical Society, the Society of Automotive Engineers, and the International Committee on Alcohol, Drugs and Traffic Safety. He served on the Research Council Committee on Trauma Research, the TRB Committee for the Study of Geometric Design Standards for Highway Improvements, and on the Motor Vehicle Safety Research Advisory Committee of the U.S. Department of Transportation.

Raymond C. Peck is Chief of Research of the Research and Statistics Office of the California Department of Motor Vehicles. Mr. Peck received his bachelor's and master's degrees in psychology at California State University in Sacramento. Mr. Peck has been affiliated with the Research Office of the California Department of Motor Vehicles since 1962, during which time he has conducted numerous research studies in driver training, licensing, behavior, and control. He was promoted to Chief of Research in 1984. In 1981, Mr. Peck was awarded the Human Factors Society's A.R. Lauer Award for his contributions to highway safety research. In 1983, he was corecipient of the National Highway Traffic Safety Administration's Award of Honor and Award of Merit for two papers he coauthored on traffic safety program evaluation. Mr. Peck is a member of the American Statistical Association and Western Psychological Association, and past chairman of TRB's Committee on Operator Regulation.

Thomas H. Rockwell is a Professor Emeritus of Industrial and Systems Engineering at Ohio State University and President of R&R Research, Inc., a consulting firm engaged in systems analysis and human factors engineering. Dr. Rockwell received his bachelor's degree in chemical engineering from Stanford University and his master's degree and Ph.D. in industrial and systems engineering from The Ohio State University. Dr. Rockwell has directed research on driver performance leading to over 80 theses and dissertations at Ohio State, where he has taught for more than 30 years as a Professor of Industrial and Systems Engineering. He is a member of the Ergonomics Society, a Fellow and past Member of the Executive Council of the Human Factors Society of America, a member of TRB's Committee on Vehicle User Characteristics and the Committee on the Benefits and Costs of Alternative Federal Blood Alcohol Concentration Standards for Commercial Vehicle Operators.

Robert A. Rogers is the Director of Automotive Safety Engineering for General Motors Corporation. Mr. Rogers received his bachelor of science in mechanical engineering from Michigan State University. He joined General Motors in 1953 and has held positions of increasing responsibility, from head of crash testing and field accident investigation activities at the Safety Research and Development Laboratory to technical liaison with the federal government on vehicle safety matters to Executive Engineer for Automotive Safety Engineering with responsibility for coordination of rulemaking and compliance issues to Director of Automotive Emission Control with responsibility for mobile emissions and fuel economy coordination. Mr. Rogers is a member of the Society of Automotive Engineers, past Chairman of the Vehicle Safety Development Subcommittee of the Motor Vehicle Manufacturers Association, and a member of the Association for the Advancement of Automotive Medicine. In 1987 he was appointed to the Motor Vehicle Safety Research Advisory Committee of the National Highway Traffic Safety Administration to advise the Administrator on automotive safety research needs.

Maxine L. Savitz is Director of Garret Ceramic Components of Allied Signal Aerospace Company. She received her bachelor's degree from Bryn Mawr College and her Ph.D. in organic chemistry from the Massachusetts Institute of Technology. Dr. Savitz has held several positions as a manager of large research programs. She was a program manager for the National Science Foundation's program of Research Applications to

National Needs, Deputy Assistant Secretary for Conservation at the U.S. Department of Energy, and President of the Lighting Research Institute. Dr. Savitz is a member of the Energy Engineering Board and the National Materials Advisory Board of the National Academy of Sciences as well as a member of the American Academy of Arts and Sciences and the American Chemical Society.

John J. Zogby is the Deputy Secretary for Safety Administration at the Pennsylvania Department of Transportation (PennDOT), where he oversees the functions of the Bureau of Motor Vehicles, the Bureau of Driver Licensing, and the Center for Highway Safety. He received his bachelor's degree in economics from Villanova University and his master's degree in public administration from Pennsylvania State University. Mr. Zogby held numerous positions at PennDOT before assuming his current position as Deputy Secretary, including Director of the Bureau of Accident Analysis, State Traffic Records Coordinator, and Chief of the Accident Investigation Section of the Bureau of Traffic Engineering. Mr. Zogby is a member of the Institute of Transportation Engineers, the Highway Safety Committee of the American Association of State Highway and Transportation Officials, and the Traffic Division of the National Safety Council. He is the Governor's Highway Safety Representative for Pennsylvania and past President of the American Association of Motor Vehicle Administrators for Region 1. He is Chairman of TRB's Committee on Planning and Administration of Transportation Safety.